VICENZA TRAVEL G

Comprehensive guide to Vicenza food and wine, accommodation, when to visit, how to get around and travel planning 2023.

Rebecca J. William

TABLE OF CONTENT

INTRODUCTION

Vicenza is a beautiful city with a long history and classic appeal, located in the scenic region of Veneto in Italy. Vicenza's attractiveness stems from its amazing architectural treasures, cultural heritage, and creative wonders, which span its history from its early Roman origins to the golden age of the Renaissance. You'll be mesmerized by the masterpieces of the legendary architect Andrea Palladio, who adorned the cityscape with elegance and sophistication, as you stroll along its cobblestoned streets.

The Basilica Palladiana, the Teatro Olimpico, and the Villa Capra "La Rotonda" are just a few examples of the architectural wonders that showcase the history of the city. Vicenza is renowned for its impressive collection of museums and galleries that highlight its artistic legacy, therefore its cultural relevance goes beyond its structures.

Priceless art collections that provide an insight into the artistic heritage of the city are housed in the Museo Civico and Gallerie di Palazzo Leoni Montanari. The city also has a thriving contemporary art culture, with lively galleries that showcase its contemporary creative spirit.

Vicenza has a unique charm thanks to its local secrets and hidden treasures, in addition to its historical and cultural resources. Explore quaint areas, hidden gardens, and artisanal goods that highlight the city's regional customs and workmanship by venturing off the usual route.

Vicenza is enthralling for its urban splendor, but its environs are as beautiful. A beautiful getaway from the bustle of the city, the Veneto countryside provides a gorgeous scenery of vineyards, undulating hills, and elegant houses. It is essential to see the Venetian Villas, which are part of the UNESCO World Heritage Site and provide an opportunity to experience the luxury of medieval estates amidst breathtaking scenery.

Vicenza comes alive all year long with exciting festivals and activities that honor its customs and culture. The city offers a dynamic atmosphere that entices guests to participate in the celebrations, from customary festivals with colorful parades to the melodic songs of the Vicenza Jazz Festival.

Without enjoying Vicenza's wonderful cuisine, of course, no trip there would be complete. Enjoy delectable pasta meals, delectable risottos, and divine tiramisu while experiencing the warmth of Italian hospitality to experience the delicacies of the Veneto area.

Vicenza is more than just a place; it is a journey through time that creates a beguiling tapestry of natural beauty and cultural richness. Vicenza is guaranteed to create a lasting impression on your heart and spirit, whether you're an art aficionado, a history buff, or just looking for an intriguing location. Prepare to get swept up in Vicenza's attraction, a city that begs you to discover its beauties and revel in its enduring beauty.

Vicenza history and culture

Vicenza is a city with a long history that dates all the way back to the Roman Empire. It has been shaped over time by a number of civilizations, leaving traces of their historical significance that may still be seen in the architecture and cultural attractions.

Vicenza experienced its heyday during the Renaissance, when world-famous architect Andrea Palladio permanently altered the city's landscape. The Basilica Palladiana, Teatro Olimpico, and Villa Capra "La Rotonda" are just a few examples of Palladio's masterpieces that continue to astound visitors with their timeless elegance. His innovative architectural designs, influenced by classical Roman principles, have given Vicenza the moniker "City of Palladio."

The city is significant in terms of culture beyond architecture because it proudly displays its artistic legacy in a number of museums and galleries. The magnificent collection of paintings, sculptures, and antiques on display at the Museo Civico provides a window into Vicenza's cultural heritage. An additional cultural treasure that showcases a variety of works of art and exhibitions that honor the city's artistic culture is the Gallerie di Palazzo Leoni Montanari.

Vicenza has always been a center of trade and commerce, which has contributed to its international feel and friendliness. Due to the city's advantageous location across significant trade routes, several civilizations came together, creating a distinctive fusion of traditions and practices that the residents still uphold today.

The picturesque neighborhoods of Vicenza, each with their own personality and history to share, are where one may feel the historical significance of the city. As one strolls around the streets and squares, one can see remnants of the past everywhere, including historic buildings and monuments.

Vicenza's Venetian Villas are a testament to the city's cultural significance and have been listed as a UNESCO World Heritage Site. These sumptuous villas, which are dispersed throughout the Veneto countryside, serve as a reminder of the area's aristocratic heritage and its seamless blending with the environment.

Festivals and cultural events in the city boost its dynamism and sense of belonging. Traditional celebrations like the Festa dei Santi Apostoli and the Palio di Vicenza unite locals and tourists to celebrate long-standing traditions.

Due to Vicenza's rich history and cultural significance, the city has successfully merged its historical past with a contemporary and vibrant present. Vicenza offers visitors an enriching experience that reveals the character of this alluring Italian gem. This includes everything from its architectural marvels to its cultural riches and festive traditions.

Geography and climate

Vicenza is distinguished by its varied landscape and comfortable climate. It is located around 60 kilometers west of Venice and is surrounded by undulating hills and lush surroundings. A great starting point for exploring the lovely Veneto countryside is the city's location.

The region's proximity to the Alps and the Adriatic Sea affects its climate. Vicenza has four unique seasons, each of which has its own allure. The summers are typically sunny and pleasant, with an average temperature of 25 to 30 degrees Celsius (77 to 86 degrees Fahrenheit). The weather is ideal for taking part in outdoor activities and discovering the city's cultural attractions.

The mild and pleasant weather of spring and fall make these seasons well-liked for tourists. The city's charm is enhanced by the springtime blooms and the autumnal foliage's golden tones. It's a fantastic time to explore the cobblestoned streets, find hidden treasures, and take advantage of the outdoor cafes.

Vicenza experiences comparatively warm winters, with lows of 0 to 10 degrees Celsius and highs of 32 to 50 degrees Fahrenheit. Although it is uncommon, during the coldest months there may be a coating of snow on the nearby hills. Wintertime provides a more serene and uncrowded experience that is ideal for experiencing the quaint environment and regional customs of the city.

The city is traversed by the Brenta River, which adds to its natural beauty and offers a tranquil setting for strolls along the riverbanks. In addition, travelers can discover these spectacular natural beauties thanks to Vicenza's advantageous location between the Dolomites and Lake Garda, further diversifying the city's geography.

The geographic landscape and climate of Vicenza provide visitors a magical environment. The city offers a beautiful blend of urban charm and natural beauty all year long, from its verdant surroundings to its temperate climate. Vicenza guarantees a wonderful experience in the embrace of its varied topography and welcoming atmosphere, whether seeing the city's historic landmarks or traveling into the lovely countryside.

Why visit Vicenza?

Vicenza is a charming destination with a distinctive blend of history, culture, and natural beauty. The famous architect Andrea Palladio had an impact on the city's rich architectural history, which offers a fascinating journey through time. From the Teatro Olimpico to the Basilica Palladiana, every nook emanates ageless beauty and artistic marvels.

The Veneto region is a welcoming vacation destination all year round because to its temperate climate and varied topography. While spring and autumn exhibit the beauty of budding flowers and golden leaves, summers provide bright, sunny days for outdoor exploration. The temperate temperatures allow for a comfortable and peaceful atmosphere even in the winter.

Vicenza's museums, galleries, and events honoring its artistic past demonstrate the city's cultural importance.

While local festivals animate the city with vivid customs and joyous celebrations, the Museo Civico and Gallerie di Palazzo Leoni Montanari exhibit priceless art collections.

Beyond the urban appeal, Vicenza's surrounding countryside in the Veneto region is a treasure trove of unspoiled beauty. The scenic escape is made possible by the undulating hills, vineyards, and Venetian villas, which offer the ideal fusion of history and environment.

Every tourist feels a sense of belonging because to the city's kind hospitality and cozy atmosphere. Vicenza offers a genuine feeling of Italian living, whether it be through exploring obscure neighborhoods, enjoying regional cuisine, or indulging in cultural experiences.

All types of travelers can expect a captivating and educational experience when visiting Vicenza. Vicenza's attraction will leave you with lasting memories and a want to return again and again, regardless of whether you're an art fan, a history buff, a nature enthusiast, or simply looking for an escape into Italian charm.

What to bring home from your trip to Vicenza

You can appreciate Vicenza's charm and cultural legacy long after your visit by taking mementos home with you. The city has a wonderful selection of gifts and souvenirs that are heartfelt keepsakes.

Handmade Items:

- Vicenza is renowned for its talented craftspeople who create exquisite items including leather goods, handmade glassware, and ceramics. These distinctive items display the city's skilled craftsmanship and creative flare.

Souvenirs with a Palladian flair:

- Embrace the city's architectural treasures by bringing home small models or prints of well-known Palladian structures like the Basilica Palladiana or Villa Capra "La Rotonda."

Olive oil and local wine:

- Both the wines and olive oils produced in the Veneto region are superb. You can take a taste of the terroir of the area with you by bottling some of these flavors.

Memorabilia from Venetian Villas:

- Search the area for books, postcards, or calendars that showcase the magnificent Venetian Villas. These things perfectly portray the appeal of these UNESCO-listed old manor houses.

Italian cuisine:

- Stock up on regional delicacies like aged cheese, artisanal pasta, and traditional pastries like panettone and amaretti biscuits.

Locally produced crafts:

- Look for locally produced goods like lace, woven baskets, or woodcarvings. These products highlight the area's rich artisanal history.

Jewelry from Vicenza:

- Vicenza, a city renowned for its goldsmithing heritage, has a range of chic jewelry and accessories that make for classic souvenirs.

Posters and art prints:

- To find prints and posters of well-known paintings or artworks influenced by Vicenza's cultural past, visit art galleries or gift shops.

Authentic Finds:

- Find one-of-a-kind antiques that represent a piece of Vicenza's past by perusing neighborhood antique shops or flea markets.

Lavender-related goods:

- The lavender fields in the area are well recognized. For a bit of Provencal charm, bring back items like soaps, sachets, or essential oils that are steeped with lavender.

To ensure a hassle-free trip home with your prized Vicenza souvenirs, always check customs procedures and travel limitations before purchasing anything, especially if you're buying food or plants.

CHAPTER 1

Travel Planning

To get the most out of your trip, careful planning and preparation are necessary when visiting Vicenza. Here are some tips to make sure your journey is easy-going and enjoyable:

Study & Learn:

- Start by learning about the city's sights, landmarks, and cultural activities. To truly understand Vicenza's significance, become familiar with its past and architectural legacy.

Pick the Right Moment:

- Take into account the ideal time to go based on your preferences. While spring and fall are known for their moderate temperatures and sparser crowds, summers offer sunny weather and bustling festivities.

Organize a schedule:

- Plan your day's activities, making sure to include must-see locations like the Teatro Olimpico and Basilica Palladiana. Combine cultural excursions with free time to discover hidden gems and take in the atmosphere of the place.

Reserve lodging in advance:

- To guarantee availability and get the best discounts, book your accommodations as soon as possible, especially during the busiest travel times.

Pack appropriately:

- Pack clothing appropriate for the season after consulting the weather forecast. For touring the city's lovely streets, remember to bring some comfortable walking shoes.

Smart Spending:

- Establish your travel budget, taking into account costs for lodging, travel, meals, and attractions.

Search for affordable solutions without sacrificing the standard of your experience.

Basic Italian Phrases to Learn:
- Despite the fact that most people there understand English, learning a few basic Italian words will improve your trip and demonstrate that you value the local way of life.

Think about guided tours:
- Your comprehension of Vicenza can be enhanced by taking part in guided tours or hiring local guides, who can offer insightful information about the city's history and architecture.

Eat local food:
Taste regional specialties and traditional cuisine. To experience the original flavors of the Veneto area, look for genuine trattorias and marketplaces.

Make Room for Unpredictability:

Plan ahead, but leave some room for improvisation. Finding unanticipated encounters and hidden jewels frequently gives your journey a distinctive touch.

Observe regional customs:

- Respect the culture and the people you meet by becoming familiar with their rituals and traditions.

By using these tips, you may plan an enjoyable trip to Vicenza where you can immerse yourself in the city's fascinating history, art, and culture and take advantage of the country's legendary hospitality.

The best time to visit Vicenza

Depending on your interests and the experience you're looking for, there is no one optimum time to visit Vicenza. You can customize your trip to fit your interests because each season has its own allure.

Summertime (June to August)

Due to its pleasant and sunny weather, summer is one of the most popular seasons to visit Vicenza. Vibrant festivals, outdoor activities, and energetic street performances bring the city to life. It's a great time to take in the city's vibrant atmosphere, tour the city's historical sites, and dine al fresco.

Spring (March to May)

Vicenza's spring weather is moderate, and the flowering flowers create a gorgeous and alluring scene. The city is less busy than it is during the height of summer, which makes it perfect for leisurely strolls, discovering hidden attractions, and taking in the local culture without the crowds.

Fall (September to November)

As the number of tourists declines, autumn offers excellent weather and a more tranquil atmosphere. Warm colors adorn the area around the city, making it a lovely time to travel into the Veneto countryside and discover the charming vineyards and ancient villas.

Winter (December to February).

Vicenza experiences a reasonably warm winter with few below-freezing days. Even though there are less tourists in the city at this time of year, it still has a warm and peaceful ambiance that is ideal for touring museums, dining on regional food, and taking in the city's genuine beauty.

The best season to visit Vicenza ultimately relies on your particular choices, including whether you enjoy the summer's exuberant energy, the spring's flowering beauty, the autumn's warm colors, or the winter's tranquil atmosphere. Vicenza is a beautiful destination all year round and provides a thrilling experience loaded with history, art, and culture in every season.

Visa Requirement

Depending on your country of citizenship and the length of your stay, you may need a visa to enter Vicenza. Italy is a member of the Schengen Area, which permits citizens of specific nations to travel without a visa for brief visits (often up to 90 days within a 180-day period).

You can enter Vicenza and remain there for up to 90 days if you are a citizen of a Schengen Area nation. But you must have a passport that is current and has at least three months left on it after your intended departure date.

You might need to apply for a Schengen Visa if you're a citizen of a non-Schengen nation in order to visit Vicenza. Whether you are visiting for business, pleasure, or family will determine the sort of visa you need.

The following paperwork is normally required in order to apply for a Schengen Visa:

A finished visa application, Passport must be current, have at least two blank pages, and be valid for at least three months after the date of your intended departure. Recent passport-size pictures that fulfill the necessary specifications.

Evidence indicating trip plans, such as a flight schedule and hotel reservations.

Travel health insurance that pays for medical costs and repatriation while you're inside the Schengen Zone.

Please provide evidence of your ability to sustain yourself during your visit, such as bank statements or a letter from a sponsor.
An itinerary outlining the activities you have scheduled while visiting Vicenza.

To prove your intention to return, you must provide evidence of ties to your home country, such as work or property ownership.

It's crucial to confirm the precise visa specifications for your nation of residence and make arrangements in advance to enable enough time for the visa application process.

To guarantee a smooth and trouble-free journey to Vicenza, always double-check the most recent visa policies and entrance requirements with the Italian embassy or consulate in your country before making travel arrangements.

Money and currency matter

To ensure a successful and pleasurable vacation, it's crucial for visitors to Vicenza to be knowledgeable about the local currency and financial issues.

Currency:

- Italy uses the Euro (EUR) as its official currency. Vicenza and the rest of the nation utilize it, and the sign for it is €. To prevent confusion during transactions, make sure you are familiar with the Euro denominations and their appearance.

Cards and Cash:

- Although Vicenza accepts credit and debit cards frequently, it's a good idea to have some cash on hand, particularly for minor transactions and in locations where card payments might not be accepted. There are many ATMs (bancomats) in the city where you may use your debit card to withdraw Euros.

Inform Your Bank:

- Give your bank advance notice of your trip to Vicenza to prevent any problems with your cards while you're overseas. If your bank is unaware of your vacation plans, it may prohibit international transactions for security reasons.

Exchange rates:

- Keep up with the exchange rates between the Euro and your own currency. Banks, exchange bureaus, and airports all offer currency exchange services. However, using your debit card to get Euros from an ATM is frequently more economical.

Fees for Foreign Transactions:

- In order to avoid paying any international transaction fees when using your card in Italy, check with your bank. Some banks could tack on a small fee or percentage to every international transaction.

Tipping:

- Italy does not use tips as frequently as some other nations. It is not required, but it is appreciated, especially for outstanding service. If you want to tip, it's traditional to round up the bill or leave a few euros.

Security and Safety:

- While exploring the city, keep your money, cards, and valuables locked up. If you're in a crowded place and you want to prevent theft or pickpocketing of your things, think about utilizing a money belt or a safe travel wallet.

You may handle your financial transactions with ease and thoroughly enjoy your time touring the beautiful city of Vicenza without any worries if you keep these currency and money problems in mind.

Language and communicating

Understanding the language and manner of communication as a first-time visitor to the fascinating city of Vicenza will substantially improve your trip experience. While English is frequently used throughout Vicenza, even though Italian is the country's official language, especially in tourist hotspots and enterprises. However, learning a few fundamental Italian phrases can surely improve your conversations and show that you appreciate the community.

People in Vicenza are friendly and inviting, and they welcome it when visitors try to speak Italian. Consider memorizing a few key words and phrases before departing, such as "buongiorno" (good morning),

Thank you "grazie"

"per favore" (please) is used, and

"Scusa" is Spanish for "excuse me."

The locals will reply to your greetings and pleasantries with sincere warmth and thanks, so use them to start conversations.

You might strike up conversations with shopkeepers, waiters, or other travelers as you stroll through Vicenza's picturesque streets, marketplaces, and cafes. Accept the use of hand gestures, which are common in Italy and help to express oneself more effectively. When overcoming communication obstacles and building relationships, a simple smile and nod can go a long way.

It's a good idea to bring a compact pocket dictionary or use language translation applications on your smartphone even if English is often spoken, particularly in hotels, museums, and popular tourist destinations. These resources can come in handy for understanding menus, signs, and other sporadic language barriers.

Italians in the area are well known for their friendliness and desire to help tourists. Never be afraid to approach the locals with a friendly "mi scusi" (excuse me) and ask for assistance if you require instructions or suggestions. Most will be happy to offer advice and may even take satisfaction in highlighting the best parts of their city.

It's polite to use formal terminology and titles in formal situations or while talking with officials, such as "Signore" (Mr.) and "Signora" (Mrs.), until invited to use first names. The Italian way of life places a high priority on politeness and respect.

Finally, embrace the Italian philosophy of "la dolce vita" (the pleasant life) and let the atmosphere of the city envelop you. Take the time to appreciate regional cuisine, converse with residents and other tourists, and take in Vicenza's colorful culture because Italians value unhurried meals and social connections.

Even though English is widely spoken in Vicenza, learning a few fundamental Italian words and phrases will help you interact with the locals more effectively and have more rewarding experiences. Vicenza will make your trip an exciting adventure of cultural exploration and sincere human interactions thanks to the city's warm welcome and admiration for your efforts.

Stay Permit

Understanding the requirements for a stay permit is crucial for first-time visitors to Vicenza in order to guarantee a smooth and lawful stay in Italy. You can enter Italy, including Vicenza, without a visa if you are a national of a Schengen member state for brief stays of up to 90 days within a 180-day window. Your passport must be valid for at least three months after the day you intend to depart.

If your visit is shorter than 90 days, you don't need to apply for a separate stay permit or visa when you arrive in Italy, including Vicenza. But it's important to keep track of how many days you spend there because going over your allotted time can result in fines, expulsion, or future travel restrictions.

Before your 90-day visa-free stay expires, you may need to apply for a residency permit (Permesso di Soggiorno) if you intend to stay in Vicenza longer than that or for reasons other than tourism. For extended stays in Italy for employment, school, family reunion, or other purposes, a residence visa is necessary.

Prior to traveling to Vicenza, it is crucial for nationals of non-Schengen Area nations, such as those from the United States, Canada, Australia, or a variety of other nations, to apply for a Schengen Visa. Whether you are traveling for business, pleasure, or a family vacation will determine the sort of visa you require. Depending on your country of citizenship, the particular requirements and application process for Schengen Visas may change. These visas typically permit stays of up to 90 days throughout a 180-day period.

You will ordinarily have to go to the Italian embassy or consulate in your native country to submit an application for a resident permit or a Schengen Visa. A valid passport, passport-sized pictures, travel medical insurance, the ability to sustain yourself financially during your stay, and any other supporting documentation required based on the purpose of your trip may be required as part of the application process.

Planning ahead and giving yourself enough time to apply for a visa or residency permit before your intended travel dates is crucial. Learn about the regulations that are specific to your country of citizenship and reason for stay because being prepared in advance will help you avoid any problems or delays at the last minute.

Understanding the requirements for a stay permit is essential for first-time visitors to Vicenza in order to have a legal and trouble-free stay in Italy. For brief stays of up to 90 days, citizens of Schengen Area nations are exempt from needing a visa. A Schengen Visa is often required for non-citizens of the Schengen Area, and a residence permit could be needed for longer periods. To guarantee a smooth and pleasurable trip to Vicenza, always confirm the most recent visa and residency permit requirements with the Italian embassy or consulate in your country.

Travel insurance

Prioritizing travel insurance as a first-time visitor to Vicenza is crucial for a worry-free and safe journey. Travel insurance offers important protection against unanticipated events that could happen while you are traveling, bringing you financial stability and peace of mind.

The following essential factors should be taken into account while choosing travel insurance for your Vicenza trip:

Medical Protection:

- Make sure your travel insurance covers extensive medical care, including hospitalization, emergency medical costs, and, if necessary, medical repatriation back to your home country. Despite Italy's top-notch healthcare system, uninsured travelers may find their medical bills to be prohibitively expensive.

Cancellation & Interruption of a Trip:

- If you need to cancel or shorten your trip because of unplanned circumstances like illness, injury, or family emergency, look for insurance that offer coverage. This insurance can assist in reimbursing pre-paid travel expenses, such as lodging and airfare.

Baggage lost or delayed:

- Make sure your insurance covers delayed, lost, or stolen baggage. This will provide reimbursement for any necessary products you might have to buy in the event that your luggage is temporarily lost.

Missed connections and delays during travel:

- Travel delays and missed connections should be covered by travel insurance, which can assist in defraying additional costs for lodging, meals, and transportation in the event of unanticipated airline delays or interruptions.

Personal Responsibility:

- Consider purchasing insurance with personal liability protection to cover any legal costs you may incur if you unintentionally harm or damage someone else while traveling.

Services for Emergency Assistance:

- Search for insurance companies that give round-the-clock emergency help. These services can be extremely helpful in case of a medical emergency, or if you need help with misplaced documents or travel-related problems.

Coverage of Adventure Activities:

- Make sure your insurance covers any adventurous activities you intend to partake in while visiting Vicenza, such as trekking or skiing, to prevent coverage gaps.

Review the policy terms, coverage limitations, and exclusions thoroughly before getting travel insurance to be sure it satisfies your unique demands and travel schedule. To get the finest policy that provides thorough coverage at an affordable price, compare various insurance providers.

An important consideration while organizing your first vacation to Vicenza is travel insurance. It offers essential safety and financial support in the event of unforeseen circumstances, ensuring you may completely enjoy your journey in security and confidence. By purchasing travel insurance, you can concentrate on discovering Vicenza's charming city while having a safety net in place for any unforeseen problems that may happen.

CHAPTER 2

Getting to Vicenza

Y ou can easily and conveniently go to this fascinating location, where you can begin a memorable trip through history, culture, and unspoiled natural beauty. Vicenza offers a variety of well-connected transportation alternatives that will guarantee a smooth and enjoyable trip whether you decide to travel by car, rail, or airplane.

Air

Travelers traveling in Vicenza for the first time may find it more convenient and effective to fly. The closest significant international airport to Vicenza is Venice Marco Polo Airport (VCE), which is situated about 70 kilometers to Vicenza's west.

Depending on the flight schedule and distance, the time of departure and arrival from various countries may change. For instance, it often takes 2 to 3 hours for planes from major European cities like London, Paris, Berlin, and Amsterdam to arrive at Venice Marco Polo Airport.

Airport's address:

Marco Polo Airport in Venice, Italy's Viale Galileo Galilei, 30/1, Tessera, 30173.

Telephone: +39 041 260 9260.

Tourists can reach Vicenza via a variety of modes of transportation after landing at Venice Marco Polo Airport. Getting a direct train from the airport to Vicenza's train station is one of the easiest possibilities. The train ride normally lasts one to one and a half hours and provides beautiful views of the Veneto region.

Visitors also have the option of renting a car or taking a cab from the airport to Vicenza. The airport offers car rentals, giving you the freedom to explore the city and its surroundings at your own speed.

Flight prices to Venice Marco Polo Airport might change depending on the point of departure, the time of year, and the booking window. In general, flexible travel dates and early reservations might result in more economical flight options. To select the most convenient and economical flight for your vacation, it is necessary to check prices across several airlines and travel websites.

I advise you to think about the flying options that fit your needs and price range the best. Vicenza is easily reachable from Venice Marco Polo Airport, providing a seamless transition into the city's alluring charm and enabling you to start an educational adventure through history, art, and culture.

Train

Train travel provides a real Italian travel experience and is convenient and beautiful. The city is easily accessible from many European locations thanks to its excellent train connections to the Italian rail network.

The travel time by train to Vicenza varies from major cities. For instance, the rail ride takes between two and three hours from Rome, Milan, Florence, and Venice, depending on the type of train and the point of departure.

The experience for visitors at Vicenza's train station should be seamless and delightful. The station's central location makes it simple to reach lodgings, famous sites, and cultural attractions.

Station for trains: 37 Viale della Stazione, Vicenza VI, 36100, Italy
Website: www.trenitalia.com
Telephone: +39 892 021

The train station's transportation alternatives are easily accessible and well-organized. Taxis are easily accessible right outside the station, offering rapid access to hotels or other locations throughout the city for customers looking for convenience.

Furthermore, automobile rental services are offered at the station or close by, enabling visitors to explore the attractive Veneto region at their own pace. In addition to operating from the station, public buses provide an affordable and effective means to go about Vicenza and its surrounds.

Tickets for trains to Vicenza range in price based on the departure station, the level of service, and the kind of train taken (such as high-speed or regional trains). It is advised to purchase train tickets in advance to lock in the lowest rates and guarantee seat availability, particularly during the busiest travel times.

I advise visitors to think about taking the train as a fun and beautiful way to go to Vicenza. Travelers may take in the magnificent scenery as they make their way to the city's architectural marvels, cultural attractions, and welcoming Italian atmosphere thanks to the Italian train network, which offers a pleasant and entertaining experience. Take advantage of the opportunity to travel like a local, and get ready to visit Vicenza, an Italian treasure with captivating beauty.

Car

Arriving in Vicenza by automobile gives first-time visitors the flexibility to explore the beautiful Italian countryside at their own speed. Driving to Vicenza offers an engaging travel experience that lets you take in the beautiful scenery along the way.

Major cities that are accessible by car from Vicenza range in size. For instance, the trip from Venice is about 70 kilometers long and takes about an hour to complete. It takes between 2.5 to 3 hours to travel the 230 kilometers from Milan, depending on traffic and the route taken.

Planning your itinerary and taking into account travel times is crucial before you set off on your trip to Vicenza. It could be a good idea to check whether there are any tolls along the road and look up rest areas or fascinating places to stop at while traveling.

When you arrive in Vicenza, there are convenient parking lots accessible. The Parking Centro Storico, which is near to the historic district and its sights, is one such choice.

The city core can usually be reached quickly from the parking lot through taxis or public transportation. Since Vicenza is a small city, many of the tourist destinations, museums, and restaurants can be reached on foot from the main parking lots.

The price of driving to Vicenza by automobile varies depending on the distance, the price of gas, and any tolls that must be paid along the way. Budgeting for your trip's fuel, parking costs, and any other costs like tolls is crucial.

While traveling to Vicenza's architectural wonders and cultural delights, you can uncover hidden gems and take in picturesque vistas by driving through the charming Italian countryside. As you travel to this alluring Italian city, embrace the freedom of the open road and get ready to make lifelong memories.

CHAPTER 3

Top Attraction

Vicenza offers a trip through time and artistic creation, from grand Palladian structures to ancient theaters and magnificent villas. Join us as we tour the city's most beautiful landmarks, each a stunning work of art that honors the ingenuity of renowned architect Andrea Palladio and the fascinating past of this Italian treasure. Prepare to be mesmerized by the beauty and allure of Vicenza's top tourist destinations, a flawless fusion of art, culture, and classic elegance.

Piazza dei Signori

Piazza dei Signori, also known as the "Square of the Lords," is one of Vicenza's most popular tourist destinations and is particularly beloved by both locals and tourists. The grandeur and significance of this ancient area make it a must-see location for tourists who are taking in the city's architectural and cultural marvels.

Address: Piazza dei Signori, 36100 Vicenza Italy

Phone: +39 0422 429999

Things to see:

Palladiana Basilica:

- Admire the magnificent façade of the Basilica Palladiana, which was created by renowned architect Andrea Palladio. Its loggia, which features massive arches and statues, is breathtaking.

Time Tower:

- Look up at the Torre Bissara clock tower that dominates the square. The square is more alluring due to its elaborate design.

The Capitaniato Palazzo:

- Admire the Palazzo del Capitaniato, a stunning structure that formerly housed the Venetian governors of the area.

Things to do:

Unwind in cafés:

- Sit at one of the quaint cafés that line the square to take in the neighborhood vibe. Enjoy a cappuccino or aperitivo as you soak in the lovely surroundings.

Watch People:

- Observe the vivid life of the city unfold in Piazza dei Signori. It's an excellent area for people-watching and immersing oneself in the local culture.

Attend Events:

- Check the schedule for events and performances held in the square, adding a touch of fun to your stay.

Guide Tips:

Visit at Different Times:

- Piazza dei Signori has a different charm during the day and night. Consider exploring it at various times to experience its changing ambience.

Historic Significance:

- Take a guided tour or learn about the square's history to comprehend its importance as a cultural and political center since Roman times.

Opening and Closing Time:

As a public square, Piazza dei Signori is open 24/7, allowing you to enjoy its splendor at any time.

Address: Piazza dei Signori, 36100 Vicenza VI, Italy.

Cost of Entry:

- Piazza dei Signori doesn't charge entry. The square is accessible to everyone, making it a wonderful place to discover and take in the history of the city.

Insight:

Piazza dei Signori is a monument to Vicenza's magnificent architecture and illustrious past. Both locals and visitors find it to be a captivating environment thanks to its well-balanced combination of famous sites and bustling atmosphere. Piazza dei Signori promises an exquisite experience that will stay with you long after you leave Vicenza, whether you visit during the day to admire its architectural intricacies or in the evening to take in the romantic ambiance.

Nearby hotel

Hotel Milano & Spa

Just 30 meters from the Verona Arena in the old district, Hotel Milano & Spa offers rooms and suites with bathrooms and color therapy, a breakfast area, supervised parking for electric vehicles, and complimentary Wi-Fi.

The fifth-floor spa has a Turkish bath, sauna, emotional shower, relaxation area, herbal tea station, and ice waterfall before ending with a jacuzzi on the outside terrace with a view of the arena for special sensory and emotional moments. The Sky Lounge Bar & Restaurant has been built with an Arena view on the fifth floor of the Hotel Milano & SPA for a memorable experience. Enjoy a delightful cocktail or a glass of champagne as a gift to yourself. Before dinner, get an aperitif, sample the menu, or have a romantic dinner after. You can reserve your event there along with a lot of other things.

Address: Vicolo Tre Marchetti 11, 37121, Verona Italy

Room types
Non-smoking rooms
Suites

Languages spoken
English, French, Russian
and Spanish

Room features
Blackout curtains
Soundproof rooms
Air conditioning

Private balcony
Room service
Coffee / tea maker
Flatscreen TV
Complimentary toiletries
Safe
Telephone
Laptop safe
Wake-up service / alarm
clock
Minibar
Refrigerator

Hair dryer

Property amenities

Valet parking

Free High Speed Internet

(WiFi)

Hot tub

Sauna

Free breakfast

Bicycle rental

Pets Allowed (Dog / Pet

Friendly)

Taxi service

Paid private parking on-

site

Wifi

Bar / lounge

Breakfast available

Breakfast buffet

Breakfast in the room

Special diet menus

Rooftop bar

Spa

Steam room

Rooftop terrace

Baggage storage

Concierge

Non-smoking hotel

Sun terrace

24-hour front desk

Dry cleaning

Laundry service

Ironing service

Nearby Restaurant

La Proseccheria - Enoteca Veneta

Location: Corso Antonio Fogazzaro 25 in pieno centro storico a 20 metri da Corso Palladio, a 70 metri da Piazza dei Signori., 36100 Vicenza Italy

Phone: +39 0444 180 3152

Price range

$6-$20

Cuisines

Italian, Wine Bar, Street Food

Special diets

Vegetarian Friendly, Vegan Options, Gluten Free Options

Meals

Lunch, Brunch, Drinks

Features

Wheelchair Accessible, Reservations, Outdoor Seating, Buffet, Seating, Serves Alcohol, Full Bar, Wine and Beer, Free Wifi, Accepts Credit Cards, Table Service, Jazz Bar

Olympic Theater

The Teatro Olimpico is a magnificent example of Renaissance theater and architecture. The grandeur, exquisite design, and historical significance of this theater make it a must-see destination.

Things to see:

Construction marvel:

- Admire the Teatro Olimpico's magnificent architecture, which was created by the renowned Andrea Palladio. A unique experience is put in motion by the theater's classically inspired façade.

Stage and Loggia:

- Admire Vincenzo Scamozzi's skillful design of the stage's ornate loggia and exquisite perspective scenery. You are transported to a compelling world of illusion by the trompe-l'oeil effects.

Things to do:

Tour Guided:

- To learn more about the theater's past and architectural significance, take a guided tour. The origins of this unique location are brought to life by knowledgeable experts.

Attend live performance

- Attend a live performance at the Teatro Olimpico if the time is right. The theater still hosts theatrical performances and concerts, offering a special chance to witness its charm in action.

Guide Advice:

Historical Relevance

- Recognize the historical significance of Teatro Olimpico, which was built in the late 16th century and served as Europe's first permanent indoor theater.

Photography:

- Take pictures of the theater's splendor, but keep in mind that flash photography is prohibited to protect the theater's fragile interiors.

Time of Opening and Closing:

- The public is often welcome to take guided tours of the Teatro Olimpico. It is advisable to call ahead for the most up-to-date schedule as opening hours are subject to change.

Address: Vicenza VI, Italy, 36100 Contra' Santa Corona.

Phone: +39 0444 321955

Website: www.teatrolimpicovicenza.it

Fee for Entry:

- Depending on the type of visit (guided tour or performance) and age category, the price of admission varies. Children and students frequently qualify for discounted rates.

Insight:

A masterpiece of architecture, the Teatro Olimpico takes guests to the splendor of the Renaissance. The theater's masterful blending of illusion and art produces a memorable experience that fully immerses you in Vicenza's rich cultural history. You will come to understand Palladio's brilliance and the continuing fascination of this great Italian gem as you enter the theater's grand loggia and investigate its beautiful stage. A trip to the Teatro Olimpico offers the chance to experience history in action and to take in the alluring atmosphere of Vicenza's creative heritage.

Opening/Closing time

6am-6pm

Nearby Hotel

Palazzo Scamozzi

Address: Corso Andrea Palladio 40, 36100 Vicenza Italy

Room types

Non-smoking rooms

Family rooms

Languages spoken

English, French, Russian and Spanish

Property amenities

Paid private parking on-site

Free High Speed Internet (WiFi)

Free breakfast

Pets Allowed (Dog / Pet Friendly)

Taxi service

Meeting rooms

Baggage storage

Newspaper

Internet

Breakfast buffet

Breakfast in the room

24-hour check-in

24-hour front desk

Laundry service

Ironing service

dryer

Room features

Blackout curtains

Air conditioning

Desk

Housekeeping

Room service

Minibar

Flatscreen TV

Bidet

Safe

Telephone

Bottled water

Clothes rack

Private bathrooms

Tile / marble floor

Wake-up service / alarm clock

Bath / shower

Complimentary toiletries

Hair

Nearby Restaurant

FuoriModena

Address: Contra San Gaetano Thiene 8, 36100 Vicenza Italy

Phone: +39 0444 330994

Price range

$6-$30

Cuisines

Italian, Mediterranean, Emilian, Northern-Italian

Meals

Dinner, Drinks

Features

Reservations, Seating, Wheelchair Accessible, Serves Alcohol, Wine and Beer, Accepts Mastercard, Accepts Visa, Accepts Credit Cards, Table Service

The Civic Museum

Since 1855, the Palazzo Chiericati has served as the Civic Museum's official residence. It now holds the city's collections of artwork from the thirteenth to the twentieth centuries, including paintings, sculptures, and decorative arts. The structure, a masterpiece of

Palladio's early development (1550), not only features embellishments from that time period but also houses significant records regarding Vicenza's art history.

After restoration work, the Palladian wing of the Museum of Palazzo Chiericati reopened in December 2013. The visitor can take in works from the sixteenth and seventeenth centuries, which were contemporaneous with the building's construction, on the main level. The Bequest of Marquis Giuseppe Roi, his personal collection of artwork from the fifteenth to the twentieth centuries, is shown in a lovely house-museum in the attic.

Visitors can view a number of masterpieces from the collection that aren't currently on display on the main level in a temporary exhibition, including works by Paolo Veneziano, Memling, Montagna, Fogolino, Sansovino, Tintoretto, Maffei, and Pittoni. The sculpture by Nereo Quagliato that was presented to the museum is housed in the basement.

Experience the fascinating worlds of art and history at Vicenza's premier tourist destination, Museo Civico. This museum, which is housed within Palazzo Chiericati, provides a fascinating tour through the cultural past of the city and has a varied collection of works of art and historical objects.

Things to see:

Artwork collections

- Admire a variety of works of art, including ornamental arts, paintings, sculptures, and works from the Middle Ages to the 19th century. A number of well-known artists, including Tiepolo and Veronese, have pieces in the museum's collection.

Historical Displays

- Investigate historical relics and archaeological discoveries that illuminate Vicenza's past and reveal the evolution and relevance of the city.

Things to do:

Guided Tour:

- Select a guided tour to learn more about the history and significance of the museum's exhibits. By revealing the collection's hidden stories and aesthetic nuance, knowledgeable guides bring history and art to life.

Attend Events:

- Consult the museum's calendar for information on cultural events, traveling exhibits, and educational activities that will make your trip more enriching.

Guide Advice:

Plan Ahead:

- To guarantee a smooth visit, research the museum's schedule and any upcoming temporary closures before you go.

Photography is typically permitted at museums, but be mindful of any restrictions and refrain from using flash to protect the artwork.

Time of Opening and Closing:

- The hours of operation for Museo Civico may change, although they are typically from Tuesday through Sunday. The most recent schedule should be found on the official website.

Address: Piazza Giacomo Matteotti 37, 36100 Vicenza Italy

Phone: +39 0444 222800

Website: www.comune.vicenza.it/museicivicivicenza

Opening/Closing time

10am-6pm

Fee for Entry:

- Museo Civico admission rates are often affordable, and children and students can enter for less money. There can be extra costs for some special exhibits or events.

Insight:

By exploring Vicenza's creative and historical legacies, Museo Civico provides a fascinating cultural experience. The museum's extensive collection takes you through several eras and gives you a full picture of the city's growth and creative accomplishments. A journey through Vicenza's cultural identity and a fuller understanding of the city's contributions to art and history can be found at Museo Civico. It's a chance to embrace Vicenza's cultural diversity and connect with the past, leaving you with cherished recollections of a completely immersive experience with the city's history.

Nearby Restaurant

Al Fiume Ristorante

Address: Contra San Paolo 2, Vicenza Italy

Phone: +39 0444 321320

Opening/Closing time

6:30pm-12am

Cuisines

Italian, Seafood, Mediterranean, European

Special diets

Vegetarian Friendly, Gluten Free Options

Meals

Lunch, Dinner

Features

Reservations, Seating, Highchairs Available, Wheelchair Accessible, Serves Alcohol, Free Wifi, Accepts Credit Cards, Table Service

Paladian basilica

A public structure facing the Piazza dei Signori is the Palladian Basilica. Its redesign by Andrea Palladio, who added the renowned loggias with serliana apertures in white marble to the old Gothic structure, is associated with the origin of its name. The Palazzo della Ragione, a Gothic-style palace constructed in the middle of the fifteenth century, was the structure on which Palladio worked.

The Council of the Four Hundred gathered in an immense chamber that occupies the entire upper floor and lacks any intermediary supports. The roof of the inverted ship's hull, copper-lined Palazzo della Ragione in Padua served as inspiration. Diamonds of red and straw-yellow Verona marble, which can still be seen behind Palladio's extension, originally covered the Gothic facade. After the structure was finished, a loggia was ordered, but construction was repeatedly delayed because of various structural issues and the condition of the ground below.

The twofold order of porticoes and loggias disintegrated towards the start of the sixteenth century, though it was not entirely destroyed. The Council enlisted the help of several prominent architects of the day to tackle the challenging issue of its rebuilding. Jacopo Sansovino, Giulio Romano, and Sebastiano Serlio were among them.

Following a competition, Andrea Palladio (1508–80) was given the project in 1549, and he continued to work on it for the remainder of his life. In 1614, it was completed after the fact. Palladio himself, who had drawn inspiration from the Roman basilica as a model for a building intended for municipal use, referred to the rebuilt structure as a basilica.

Internationally renowned architecture and art exhibitions are held in the building's three separate exhibition areas.

Experience the Basilica Palladiana, one of Vicenza's main attractions, and its magnificent architecture. This Renaissance masterpiece, created by the renowned Andrea Palladio, serves as a representation of the aesthetic brilliance and cultural history of the city.

What to see:

Beautiful Façade:

- Admire the Basilica Palladiana's imposing façade, which is embellished with elaborate sculptures and traditional Renaissance motifs and demonstrates Palladio's mastery of architectural proportions.

Loggia:

- The upper loggia of the basilica has a number of striking arches that provide panoramic views over Piazza dei Signori and the city skyline.

Thing to see:

Check out the civic museums:

- Investigate the museums located inside the basilica, which feature a varied array of works of art and artifacts from the city's past and artistic triumphs.

Scale the Terrace:

- Take an exciting climb to the rooftop terrace of the basilica, where you can admire Palladio's architectural vision and the gorgeous scenery of the city.

Guide Advice:

Tour Guided:

- Take advantage of a guided tour to learn more about the basilica's history, architectural significance, and Andrea Palladio's legacy.

Photography:

- Capture the basilica's splendor with your camera, but keep in mind to abide by any photography restrictions to protect the delicate interiors.

Time of Opening and Closing:

- The Basilica Palladiana's operating times sometimes change, so it's best to check the official website or get in touch with the basilica for the most recent schedule.

Address: Italian city of Vicenza VI, Piazza dei Signori, 36100.

Phone: +39 0444 226400

Website: www.comune.vicenza.it/palazzichiericati

Fee for Entry:

- Entry to Basilica Palladiana is often affordable, with alternatives for children's and students' reduced rates. The rooftop terrace may have an additional charge for access.

Insight:

The Basilica Palladiana is a magnificent example of Andrea Palladio's architectural brilliance and the cultural importance of Vicenza. You will be taken to a world of classic elegance and artistic brilliance as you enter the basilica's captivating interior and climb to its rooftop patio. When you visit Basilica Palladiana, you can experience history in action and learn about Palladio's lasting impact on the city's architectural heritage. You will come away from it with cherished memories of an experience with Vicenza's rich past that truly embodies the confluence of art and history.

Opening/Closing time

10am-6pm

Nearby Restaurant

La Proseccheria - Enoteca Veneta

Why pick Ev? Here are three great justifications: Life itself! "Elegant and informal" is well known. While they place a high value on elegance in every last detail, they also strive to create a relaxed atmosphere where their visitors may mingle and enjoy one another's company in an environment that embraces spontaneity and lightheartedness for people who appreciate the "Sweet Life".

That's Wine If you are an expert, you can select from more than 400 distinct labels, most of which are from Veneto, but which also have elements from the most significant wine-producing regions in Italy and, for a finishing touch, France, Germany, Austria, and New Zealand. eagerness to learn From a simple recommendation over an aperitif to a guided tasting to the discovery of their cellar, They are always available to help you explore this fascinating world. Every opportunity will be worthwhile to learn and broaden your knowledge. It is Veneto. the investigation and valuing of the area!

Address: Corso Antonio Fogazzaro 25 in pieno centro storico a 20 metri da Corso Palladio, a 70 metri da Piazza dei Signori., 36100 Vicenza Italy

Phone: +39 0444 180 3152

Website: https://www.enoteca-veneta.com

Price range

$10- $50

Cuisines

Italian, Wine Bar, Street Food

Special diets

Vegetarian Friendly, Vegan Options, Gluten Free Options

Meals

Lunch, Brunch, Drinks

Features

Wheelchair Accessible, Reservations, Outdoor Seating, Buffet, Seating, Serves Alcohol, Full Bar, Wine and Beer, Free Wifi, Accepts Credit Cards, Table Service, Jazz Bar

Santa Corona Chiesa

The Holy Thorn relic was given to the Blessed Bartolomeo da Breganze, bishop of Vicenza, by Louis IX, king of France, and is now kept in the Dominican church, which was constructed in 1261 to house it. Numerous significant paintings and sculptures are housed in the Gothic interior, which features a chancel designed by Lorenzo da Bologna in the second part of the fifteenth century.

These include the "Adoration of the Magi" by Paolo Veronese and Giovanni Bellini's masterwork "The Baptism of Christ" in the Garzadori altar, which is assigned to Rocco da Vicenza. The "Madonna of the Stars" by Lorenzo

Veneziano and Marcello Fogolino, the "Magdalen and Saints" by Bartolomeo Montagna, and the "Virgin, Child and Saints" by Giambattista Pittoni are also included. Pier Antonio dell'Abate crafted and inlaid a beautiful wooden choir for the apse. The Thiene Chapel's Michelino da Besozzo frescoes, which date from the early fifteenth century and provide a mature example of the International Gothic style, are among the building's earliest embellishments.

The Chiesa Santa Corona is a mesmerizing synthesis of spiritual devotion and aesthetic magnificence. This medieval church, one of the most popular tourist destinations in the area, provides a peaceful haven and a tour through centuries of art and architecture.

Things to see:

Last Supper:

- Admire Giovanni Bellini's beautiful work, "The Last Supper," which is on exhibit in the Cappella Maggiore. Everyone who sees the painting is enthralled by its minute details and compelling facial expressions.

A Crucifix

- Look at Andrea Palladio's wooden crucifix, which combines his skills in architecture and sculpture to create a work of stunning beauty.

Things to do:

Investigate the Chapel:

- Take your time looking through the magnificent chapel known as the Cappella Maggiore, which features frescoes, sculptures, and an amazing altar. Take a chance to reflect and think about things since the environment is peaceful.

Attend a service or Mass:

- To experience the church's spiritual significance, think about going to a mass or other religious service there if you get the chance.

Guide Advice:

Fashion Code:

When visiting Chiesa Santa Corona, keep in mind that it is a place of religion, therefore show respect by dressing modestly.

Quiet Thought:

- To truly understand the spiritual significance of the church and to provide a moment of peaceful thought, embrace the quiet atmosphere of the building.

Time of Opening and Closing:

The Chiesa Santa Corona's hours are subject to change, so it's best to check the official website or get in touch with the building's administration for the most recent timetable.

Address: Contra Santa Corona 2, 36100 Vicenza Italy

Phone: +39 0444 544395

Website: www.chiesasantacorona.it

Opening/Closing time

6am-10pm

Fee for Entry:

- Although Chiesa Santa Corona typically doesn't charge admission, donations are always appreciated to help with maintenance and conservation efforts.

Insight:

Vicenza's Chiesa Santa Corona is a veritable gold mine of historical significance and aesthetic splendor. The church is a must-see for anybody looking for an in-depth interaction with the history of the city because of its magnificent artworks, especially the outstanding "Last Supper" by Giovanni Bellini, and the profound peacefulness of its interior. You will be carried away by the profound connection between faith and art in Vicenza's cultural tapestry as soon as you enter this sacred location, which will leave you with a lasting appreciation.

Nearby Restaurant

La Proseccheria - Enoteca Veneta

Price range

$10-$20

Cuisines

Italian, Wine Bar, Street Food

Special diets

Vegetarian Friendly, Vegan Options, Gluten Free Options

Meals

Lunch, Brunch, Drinks

Features

Wheelchair Accessible, Reservations, Outdoor Seating, Buffet, Seating, Serves Alcohol, Full Bar, Wine and Beer, Free Wifi, Accepts Credit Cards, Table Service, Jazz Bar

Chapter 4

Accommodation

No matter the kind of lodging you select, a stay in Vicenza is guaranteed to be enjoyable. Each choice offers its own special character and adds to the city's attraction.

Hotels

There are accommodations to fit every traveler's taste and budget, from elegant five-star hotels to lovely boutique hotels. Vicenza's hotels offer a cozy and welcoming getaway, ensuring that your time spent in this lovely Italian city is one you won't soon forget, whether you're visiting for business, pleasure, or to discover Andrea Palladio's architectural marvels.

Campo Marzio Hotel

The Hotel Campo Marzio is conveniently located next to Corso Palladio, Piazza dei Signori, and Palazzo Chiericati, and is only 20 meters from the pedestrian area and 200 meters from Vicenza's train station. In addition to having access to bicycles for exploring the city, visitors can also choose to rent a car to travel further afield. To help visitors learn more about the customs and distinctive features of the area, the bilingual staff is happy to recommend eateries and sightseeing trips. A accessible Internet access point in the foyer and paid outdoor parking are among the amenities available. The front desk is accessible around-the-clock.

The lovely Hotel Campo Marzio is situated. The hotel provides an excellent base for experiencing the city's architectural marvels and cultural pearls because it is close to the famous Piazza dei Signori and other important sights.

Hotel Campo Marzio offers guests cozy, well-appointed rooms with a welcoming atmosphere, ensuring a comfortable and enjoyable stay. The kind and helpful team is committed to providing great service and making visitors feel at home.

The Basilica Palladiana and Teatro Olimpico, as well as surrounding dining and shopping options, are easily accessible from the hotel's prime position downtown Vicenza.

Hotel Campo Marzio provides a great experience for those looking for a comfortable and enjoyable stay in Vicenza by fusing contemporary conveniences with the city's ageless allure.

Address: Viale Roma 21, 36100 Vicenza Italy
Phone: +390444545700

Room types
City view
Non-smoking rooms
Suites
Family rooms

Room features
Soundproof rooms
Air conditioning
Room service
Safe
Minibar
Flatscreen TV

Languages spoken
English, French, German, Italian

Property amenities
Free parking
Free High Speed Internet (WiFi)
Free breakfast
Bicycle rental
Children's television networks
Pets Allowed (Dog / Pet Friendly)

Car hire	Concierge
Meeting rooms	Newspaper
Paid private parking on-site	Non-smoking hotel
	24-hour front desk
Parking	Dry cleaning
Wifi	Laundry service
Bar / lounge	Ironing service
Breakfast buffet	
Breakfast in the room	
Snack bar	
Baggage storage	

Luxurious boutique hotel

The Andrea Palladio Teatro Olimpico, the Palazzo Chiericati, and Corso Palladio, the main street, are all just 200 meters from Vicenza's Glam Boutique Hotel, which is located in the city's historical core. Free Wi-Fi is available throughout the hotel's public spaces and accommodations.

There are eight Standard Rooms, five Deluxe Rooms, and four Junior Suites at Vicenza's Glam Boutique Hotel. Each room has a minibar, Sky TV, and separate heating and cooling. Only three Junior Suites have wood floors; the remaining rooms are decorated with luxurious carpet or moquette. The vibrant, contemporary, and glamorous Glam Boutique Hotel is perfectly placed for your visit to Vicenza. Parking meters are accessible with reservations. Vicenza is your home; welcome to the Glam Boutique Hotel.

With careful attention to detail and a blend of modern aesthetics and vintage charm, the Glam Boutique Hotel boasts sleek and sophisticated rooms. To provide the highest comfort and convenience, each accommodation has been tastefully outfitted with contemporary amenities.

The attentive and welcoming staff of the Glam Boutique Hotel provides guests with first-rate service and goes above and beyond to accommodate special requests. The hotel's small-town ambience develops a customized and exclusive atmosphere that gives guests a sense of being well-cared-for.

The Glam Boutique Hotel's excellent location makes it simple for visitors to discover Vicenza's architectural wonders, historical sites, and bustling city life. The Teatro Olimpico, Piazza dei Signori, and other well-known sights are only a leisurely stroll away.

The Glam Boutique Hotel in Vicenza offers a boutique hotel experience that expertly melds luxury, flair, and individualized service. Guests are guaranteed an exceptional stay, leaving them with treasured memories of their time in this captivating Italian city.

Address: Viale Antonio Giuriolo 10, 36100 Vicenza Italy

Room types
Non-smoking rooms
Suites

Languages spoken
English, Italian

Room features
Allergy-free room
Blackout curtains
Air conditioning
Room service
Safe
Minibar
Flatscreen TV

Bath / shower

Air purifier

Bathrobes

Telephone

VIP room facilities

Bottled water

Clothes rack

Iron

Wake-up service / alarm clock

Complimentary toiletries

Hair dryer

Property amenities

Paid private parking nearby

Free High Speed Internet (WiFi)

Bar / lounge

Couples massage

Adults only

Baggage storage

Express check-in / check-out

Private check-in / check-out

Wifi

Breakfast available

Breakfast in the room

Full body massage

Massage

Neck massage

Newspaper

Non-smoking hotel

Dry cleaning

Laundry service

Ironing service

Key Hotel

The Key Hotel in Vicenza is a modern and attractive lodging that provides the ideal fusion of contemporary conveniences and Italian hospitality. Key Hotel offers a convenient base for both business and leisure tourists because to its prime location close to the city center and popular attractions.

The hotel's modern, luxurious rooms were created with a focus on both comfort and usability. Modern conveniences are provided in every room to make sure visitors have a comfortable and happy stay.

The attentive and knowledgeable personnel at Key Hotel take pleasure in their commitment to providing exceptional service and making sure that visitors have an enjoyable stay. Throughout the stay, guests feel comfortable and at ease thanks to the cozy and welcoming atmosphere.

The hotel is a great option for corporate meetings and conferences for business travelers because it has well-equipped meeting spaces and business amenities.

The hotel's restaurant offers a lovely selection of classic meals and exotic flavors, including delectable Italian food.

A fulfilling and delightful visit in this alluring Italian city is made possible by Vicenza's Key Hotel's ideal location, cozy lodgings, and first-rate service.

Address: Viale Giangiorgio Trissino 89, 36100 Vicenza Italy
Phone:+390444505476

Room types
Non-smoking rooms
Family rooms

Languages spoken
English, French, Spanish and German

Hotel style
Green
Business

Room features
Soundproof rooms
Air conditioning

Desk

Private balcony

Room service

Flatscreen TV

Bath / shower

Hair dryer

Safe

Telephone

Baggage storage

Concierge

Street parking

Wifi

Bar / lounge

Breakfast available

Breakfast buffet

Breakfast in the room

Property amenities

Free parking

Free High Speed Internet (WiFi)

Free breakfast

Bicycle rental

Children's television networks

Solarium

Vending machine

Newspaper

Non-smoking hotel

Shared lounge / TV area

Sun terrace

24-hour front desk

Dry cleaning

Laundry service

Ironing service

Vicenza hotel antico

The hotel is situated in the Stradella dei Nodari, a busy pedestrian area close to Piazza dei Signori, one of the most significant and historic hotels in the city's center. Great performers who were appearing at the Teatro Olimpico at the turn of the 20th century are known to have stayed at the hotel. The artists have been mesmerized by the terrace with a stunning view of the city's roofs as well as by the main, elegant staircase that connects the entry and the upper floors, typical of the old palaces.

The ancient, four-story structure from the early 20th century offers 23 rooms total, including 4 suites and 8 junior suites. A panoramic terrace is located on the fifth floor, from which you can take in the breathtaking views of Monte Berico, the Little Dolomites, the San Giacomo Church, the Santo Stefano Dome, and San Vincenzo. Due to its distinctive green color in the middle of the city, you can easily identify the Basilica Palladiana.

These stunning structures are both Vicenza's icons and masterpieces by Vicenza's famed architect Andrea Palladio. SERVICES The Antico Hotel Vicenza is the ideal spot for a stress-free getaway because of its elegance, flair, and knowledgeable personnel. The American breakfast buffet offers a wonderful assortment of regional goods to sample and the ideal way to start your day. If you want to have a coffee or a drink of wine while perusing a book from our library, the bar is always open. You can always snap pictures of the scenery from the terrace, and in the summer you may have dinner or have an aperitif there. - concierge service - multilingual - free wifi - safe - left-luggage office Reading room and lift - Morning meal -Bar - Coffee and tea making facilities Room service breakfast is available upon request from 7:00am to 10:00am. Breakfast is served on the terrace from 7 to 10 a.m. - Laundry service - Personal trainer - Beauty aide - Hairdresser - Rent a bike - Rent a high-end vehicle - Covered parking • Rental of the expansive patio exclusively - Airport shuttle service - Transfer to/from fair - Small pets (6 kg maximum)

With their classic decor and antique furnishings, the Antico Hotel Vicenza's charmingly appointed rooms bring back fond memories. Each room is intended to be a welcoming haven where visitors can recover after a day of touring the city.

The hotel's prime location makes it simple for visitors to reach Vicenza's well-known sights, including the Basilica Palladiana and Piazza dei Signori, as well as nearby eateries, shopping, and cultural hubs.

The welcoming staff of Antico Hotel Vicenza makes sure each visitor has a unique and enjoyable stay. The helpful staff is always there to help with any inquiries or suggestions to maximize the Vicenza experience.

The Antico Hotel Vicenza provides a beautiful fusion of old-world charm and contemporary conveniences for guests seeking a distinctive and historic stay in Vicenza, making it an ideal option for tourists hoping to experience the city's enduring fascination.

Address: Stradella Dei Nodari n° 5, 36100 Vicenza Italy
Phone: +3904441573422

Room types
Non-smoking rooms   Hotel style
Family rooms   Classic

Charming

Languages spoken

English, French, Russian
and Spanish

Room features

Air conditioning

Housekeeping

Private balcony

Minibar

Flatscreen TV

Property amenities

Paid public parking
nearby

Free High Speed Internet
(WiFi)

Free breakfast

Children Activities (Kid /
Family Friendly)

Pets Allowed (Dog / Pet
Friendly)

Shuttle bus service

Rooftop terrace

Baggage storage

Street parking

Wifi

Bar / lounge

Breakfast buffet

Breakfast in the room

Rooftop bar

Concierge

Newspaper

Non-smoking hotel

24-hour front desk

Dry cleaning

Laundry service

Inns with breakfasts

Vicenza's bed and breakfasts provide a pleasant and private opportunity to explore the elegance and warmth of the city. These B&Bs offer a special chance to become immersed in the customs and culture of the area because they are tucked away among the scenic streets and old neighborhoods.

In contrast to larger hotels, Vicenza's bed and breakfasts often provide a more individualized experience, with attentive hosts ready to share their local expertise and suggest off-the-beaten-path gems.

These quaint lodgings frequently occupy ancient structures, adding to the authenticity and fostering a welcoming atmosphere for visitors. B&Bs in Vicenza provide cozy accommodations and hearty breakfasts that highlight regional delicacies, ensuring a wonderful stay that perfectly captures the spirit of this alluring Italian city. A stay at a Vicenza bed and breakfast guarantees a singular and enlightening experience, leaving you with priceless memories of your time in this cultural treasure, whether you're visiting for business or pleasure.

Vicenza's Portico Rosso B&B

Within Vicenza's ancient city walls is the 15th-century villa that now serves as Portico Rosso Bed & Breakfast. At Portico Rosso, each elegantly furnished room has parquet flooring, wood ceiling beams, new cotton and linen bedding, and contemporary amenities. The private bathroom in Room DIANA has a spa bath and a shower and gives a view of the garden. A hairdryer and complimentary toiletries are provided in each bedroom. They provide a lovely private garden in a calm, refined, and informal setting. There is free WiFi everywhere. Every day, they serve a traditional Italian breakfast that includes pastries, hot beverages, and fresh fruit juice.

If the weather is nice, guests can eat their meal in the private garden. Additionally available to guests is a communal lounge with a fireplace. (Advance notification is required for requests for particular foods.) They are a 10-minute walk from the railway station and 800 meters from

Piazza dei Signori, respectively, from the property. the A4 highway's Vicenza Ovest exit

The Portico Rosso B&B's rooms are tastefully decorated with a blend of contemporary conveniences and classic furnishings, providing a warm and welcoming atmosphere. Every amenity required for a comfortable stay is provided in each room, making visitors feel at home.

The welcoming and caring hosts of Portico Rosso B&B go above and beyond to make sure that visitors enjoy a special stay. The helpful advice and suggestions from the welcoming staff for discovering the city and its cultural assets are always accessible.

Visitors may easily discover Vicenza's architectural marvels, historical sites, and bustling local life thanks to the B&B's excellent location. Walking distance away are the Teatro Olimpico, Piazza dei Signori, and other sights.

Portico Rosso B&B is a great option for tourists looking for a home away from home since it provides a perfect blend of comfort, hospitality, and an authentically delightful stay in Vicenza.

Address: Contra San Rocco 28, 36100 Vicenza Italy

Room types

Non-smoking rooms

Family rooms

Good to know

Hotel style

Charming

Romantic

Languages spoken

English, Spanish, Italian

Room features

Air purifier

Air conditioning

Desk

Housekeeping

Private balcony

Coffee / tea maker

Extra long beds

Bidet

Safe

Sofa

Wardrobe / closet

Bottled water

Clothes rack

Private bathrooms

Tile / marble floor

Electric kettle

Whirlpool bathtub

Bath / shower

Complimentary toiletries

Hair dryer

Property amenities

Free public parking
nearby

Baggage storage

Non-smoking hotel

Free High Speed Internet
(WiFi)

Wifi

Breakfast available

Hot tub

Breakfast in the room

Free breakfast

Complimentary Instant

Kids stay free

Coffee

Pets Allowed (Dog / Pet
Friendly)
/ beach chairs

Complimentary tea

Sun loungers

Bed and Breakfasts Casa Vicenza

Bed and Breakfasts Casa Vicenza is a charming and welcoming lodging option. This B&B, which is run by a friendly and inviting family, provides guests with a cozy setting and a sense of true Italian hospitality.

After a long day of exploring, guests can unwind in the Casa Vicenza's cozy, tastefully appointed rooms. Modern conveniences are provided in every room to make your stay comfortable.

The kind hosts at Casa Vicenza take great effort to put guests at ease by offering individualized service and useful suggestions to make their stay in the city more enjoyable. The welcoming and accommodating environment gives the total experience a personal touch.

The B&B's convenient location makes it simple to visit Vicenza's well-known architectural landmarks, cultural attractions, and neighborhood restaurants. The Basilica Palladiana, Piazza dei Signori, and other well-known locations are close by.

Bed & Breakfasts Casa Vicenza is a beautiful refuge that seems like a home away from home for those looking for a real and heartfelt stay in Vicenza. It's the perfect option for anyone who wants to enjoy the city's hospitality and become a part of the community.

Room types
Non-smoking rooms
Family rooms

Hotel style
Classic
Charming

Languages spoken

English, French, Russian and Spanish

Room features

Air conditioning

Housekeeping

Private balcony

Minibar

Flatscreen TV

Property amenities

Paid public parking nearby

Free High Speed Internet (WiFi)

Free breakfast

Children Activities (Kid / Family Friendly)

Pets Allowed (Dog / Pet Friendly)

Shuttle bus service

Rooftop terrace

Baggage storage

Street parking

Wifi

Bar / lounge

Breakfast buffet

Breakfast in the room

Rooftop bar

Concierge

Newspaper

Non-smoking hotel

24-hour front desk

Dry cleaning

Laundry service

Milo bed and breakfasts

The II Milo's rooms are nicely designed, providing a warm and welcoming atmosphere for visitors to unwind in. Modern conveniences are provided in every room to provide a comfortable stay.

The attentive staff at II Milo is committed to delivering individualized service and gracious hospitality, making sure that visitors feel at home and well-looked-after while they are there. Their sincere friendliness and assistance give the total experience a personal touch.

Visitors may unwind throughout their stay at the B&B thanks to its tranquil setting while still being accessible to Vicenza's famous buildings and tourist attractions. From II Milo, it is simple to reach the city's bustling core with its stunning architectural beauties.

Bed & Breakfast II Milo provides a secluded refuge with attentive hosts for tourists looking for a peaceful and picturesque getaway in Vicenza, making it a lovely option for visitors seeking a cozy and restful stay in this attractive Italian city.

Address: Strada Monte della Crocetta, 26, 36100 Vicenza Italy

Room types
Non-smoking rooms
Suites
Family rooms

Hotel style
Charming
Romantic

Languages spoken
English, French and Italian

Property amenities

Free parking
Free High Speed Internet (WiFi)
Wifi
Free breakfast
Breakfast buffet
Non-smoking hotel

Room features
Air conditioning
Desk
Kitchenette
Refrigerator
Flatscreen TV
Bath / shower
Complimentary toiletries
Hair dryer

Agriturismo

Vicenza's agriturismos provide a distinctive and genuine opportunity to take in the breathtaking Italian countryside and its agricultural heritage. Agriturismo is an Italian term that blends the pleasures of hospitality with the allure of rural life. It is derived from the words "agricoltura" (agricultural) and "turismo" (tourism).

Visitors can stay in agriturismi, historic farmhouses, or rural homes during these delightful farm stays, where they can join in agricultural activities and enjoy the gorgeous surroundings.

A peaceful retreat from the hustle and bustle of city life, agriturismo accommodations in Vicenza give visitors a chance to interact with nature and experience the local way of life. Agriturismo in Vicenza guarantees an authentic and wonderful experience that will leave you with enduring memories of the Italian countryside, whether you are picking fruits in the orchards, tasting regional wines, or simply taking in the tranquil surroundings.

Agriturismo Palazzetto Ardi's lodgings

Agriturismo Palazzetto Ardi's lodgings are elegantly furnished, fusing old-world elegance with contemporary conveniences. Comfortable lodgings with picturesque views are available to visitors, offering a tranquil haven to relax and recharge.

Visitors can become fully immersed in the local agricultural traditions thanks to the property's working farm. Visitors can experience the aromas of the regional terroir by touring the farm's vineyards and olive trees and tasting its own produce.

A wonderful visit is guaranteed by friendly hosts who share their love of the area and its riches. A personal touch is added by the family-run setting, which makes visitors feel like a member of the farm's larger family.

Agriturismo Palazzetto Ardi strikes the ideal combination between rural appeal and accessibility to the surrounding area because it provides a tranquil country escape while being conveniently close to Vicenza's historical sites and cultural attractions.

Agriturismo Palazzetto Ardi is a tranquil haven where agricultural traditions come alive for tourists looking for a genuine and immersive experience in the Vicenza countryside. Visitors leave with priceless memories of a really magical agriturismo experience.

Agriturismo Sa Michele

Vicenza's Agriturismo Sa Michele is a charming farmhouse set amidst the breathtaking Italian countryside. This agriturismo provides visitors with a tranquil and genuine retreat from the hustle and bustle of city life because it is surrounded by vineyards, olive groves, and lush surroundings.

Agriturismo Sa Michele's lodgings are intelligently constructed, fusing rustic charm with contemporary amenities. Visitors can stay in appealing rooms or flats, each of which radiates a warm and welcoming atmosphere and offers a tranquil retreat.

Agriturismo Sa Michele offers visitors the chance to observe local agricultural customs because it is a working farm. Visitors can participate in the farm's daily activities and enjoy the farm-to-table experience by partaking in wine tastings and watching the manufacture of olive oil.

Agriturismo Sa Michele's kind hosts extend a cordial welcome to visitors, providing true Italian hospitality and establishing a home away from home. Every part of the agriturismo reflects their love of the land and commitment to sustainability.

Agriturismo Sa Michele is ideally situated close to Vicenza's historic icons and attractions while being surrounded by the calm of the countryside. This makes it the perfect starting point for discovering the area's rich history and architectural marvels.

Agriturismo Sa Michele offers an unforgettable experience where nature, culture, and hospitality come together to create cherished memories of an enchanted agriturismo getaway for tourists looking for a genuine and immersive stay in the heart of Vicenza's rural splendor.

Vicenza's Agriturismo Marani

Vicenza's Agriturismo Marani is a charming country getaway that epitomizes agriturismo hospitality. The lodgings of Agriturismo Marani are created with a fusion of rustic elegance and contemporary comforts, offering visitors a warm and comfortable stay. Each lovely room or self-catering unit offers a tranquil haven for guests to unwind and relax.

Visitors can appreciate the local agricultural traditions on the farm at Agriturismo Marani. Visitors can enjoy the local flavors by strolling around the vineyards, tasting the local wines, and collecting fresh fruit from the orchards.

Agriturismo Marani's friendly and accommodating hosts offer individualized service to make visitors feel at home and well-cared for during their stay. The agriturismo experience is enhanced by their love of the land and commitment to sustainable methods.

Agriturismo Marani is perfectly located close to Vicenza's cultural icons and tourist attractions while being surrounded by the calm of the countryside. Because of this, it serves as a great starting place for discovering the area's rich historical and architectural legacy.

Agriturismo Marani offers a remarkable escape where nature, culture, and warm hospitality join together to create cherished memories of a genuinely enchanted agriturismo retreat for tourists looking for an authentic and immersive stay in the heart of Vicenza's rural charm.

CHAPTER 5

Vicenza's Festivals and Events

The festivals and events of Vicenza are a colorful tapestry of cultural celebrations that highlight the city's illustrious history and creative flair. This lovely Italian city comes alive all year long with a wide variety of festivals and events that enthrall both residents and tourists.

Vicenza's Festivals and Events promise an engaging and stimulating experience that enables you to immerse yourself in the city's dynamic culture and creative attractiveness, regardless of whether you are an art enthusiast, a music lover, a history buff, or a food explorer. These festivals and events present the heart and soul of this enchanting Italian city, showcasing everything from top-notch performances to centuries-old customs.

Vicenza Jazz Festival

An annual music spectacular honoring the rich history and diversity of jazz music is called the Vicenza Jazz Festival.

The festival, which takes place in the beautiful Italian city of Vicenza, brings together accomplished jazz musicians from all over the world to wow audiences with their passionate performances and captivating improvisations.

Event Date: The event is usually held in the summer, usually in July or August. For accurate dates and the current year's schedule, it is best to consult the festival's official website or local event listings.

Attendee Attractions:

Eclectic Jazz Performances:

- The Vicenza Jazz Festival offers a diverse selection of jazz performances that span a variety of sub-genres and styles. The event offers a diverse range of musical delights, from traditional jazz standards to modern fusion and experimental sounds.

World-class artists:

- Jazz musicians of renown deliver dazzling sets on Vicenza stages, showcasing their extraordinary skills and abiding passion for the music.

Jazz Sessions in Historic Locations:

- A few of the festival's concerts are held in Vicenza's historic locations, resulting in an atmosphere that combines the city's stunning architecture with the allure of live jazz music.

Focus on Emerging Talent:

- The festival also offers a stage for up-and-coming jazz musicians to perform, giving the audience a chance to see the future of jazz and learn about new performers.

Things to do at the Event:

Attend performances:

- Jazz lovers can fully immerse themselves in the genre by attending any of the many performances that are presented around Vicenza at various locations. Every performance promises to be different and enthralling.

Interact with Musicians:

- Jazz masterclasses and workshops are frequently held during the festival, allowing attendees to speak with accomplished musicians and learn about the subtleties of jazz improvisation and composition.

Discover the City:

- In between jazz performances, spend some time discovering Vicenza. Vicenza provides a lovely setting for the festival experience with its architectural wonders like the Palladian Basilica, vibrant local culture, and delectable Italian cuisine.

Appreciate Jazz Heritage:

- Have discussions with other jazz fans, express your passion for the music, and get a greater understanding of the cultural significance of jazz in influencing the music industry.

The Vicenza Jazz Festival is a captivating excursion into the world of jazz, where melodies and rhythms combine to produce a musical tapestry that is unforgettably beautiful.

The festival promises a harmonious celebration of jazz's everlasting attraction and its capacity to move the soul, whether you're a die-hard fan or a beginner to the genre.

Vicenza Opera Festival

The Vicenza Opera Festival is a prestigious and opulent celebration of the operatic world that highlights the magnificence of this alluring art form. The festival, which takes place in Vicenza, Italy, brings together talented opera singers, musicians, and conductors to deliver mesmerizing renditions of both traditional and modern operatic masterpieces.

Event Time:

- The event often occurs in a particular month, frequently in the summer or early fall. It is advised to check the festival's official website or local event listings for the precise dates and schedule for the current year before attending.

Attendee Attractions:

Performances of opera:

- The Vicenza Opera Festival offers viewers spellbinding opera performances that vividly depict the emotional complexity and theatrical brilliance of famous operas by different composers and eras.

World-class vocalists:

- World-class opera singers who are known for their vocal prowess and creative interpretations perform at the festival, giving each performance an extraordinary touch.

Old-time theaters

- The opera experience is enhanced by the fact that many opera performances take place in Vicenza's historic theaters, such as the Teatro Olimpico.

Present-day opera:

- The festival may feature contemporary works in addition to classic operas, providing a window into contemporary operatic compositions and advances.

Opera performances to attend:

- Attending the opera performances is the festival's principal draw. Be ready to be spellbound by the strong vocals, compelling tale, and beautiful musical accompaniment.

The Cultural Heritage of Vicenza:

- Visit Vicenza's numerous architectural marvels, such as Villa Capra "La Rotonda" and the Basilica Palladiana, between opera performances to learn more about the city's rich cultural legacy.

Attending opera workshops

- In order to give opera lovers the opportunity to learn from seasoned experts and acquire insight into the craft of opera singing and performance, the festival may host opera workshops and masterclasses.

Discuss the performance afterward:

- Post-performance discussions may be part of some performances, giving the audience an opportunity to express their opinions and have stimulating debates about the art of opera.

With its ageless craftsmanship and emotional heft, the Vicenza Opera Festival is a lavish celebration of operatic brilliance. The festival offers a magnificent voyage into the realm of music, drama, and passion, leaving you with enduring memories of this engaging cultural event whether you are an opera enthusiast or experiencing opera for the first time.

Celebration of Madonna Bruna

In the beautiful Italian city of Vicenza, there is a lively and historic Catholic celebration known as the Festa della Madonna Bruna. The event is held in honor of Madonna Bruna, Vicenza's patron saint, and is marked by a number of religious rites, processions, and exuberant parades.

Event Date:

- The event is held every year, usually in the month of July. It is advised to check the Festa della Madonna Bruna's official website or local event listings for the precise dates and schedule for the current year before attending.

Attendee Attractions:

Religious Processions:

- The statue of Madonna Bruna is carried through Vicenza's streets in a solemn and vibrant display of devotion during the festival's religious procession, which is one of its primary attractions.

Local dress:

- Locals dress in traditional costumes and attire during the festivities, bringing a sense of cultural pride and old-world charm to the festivities.

Iconic Religious Sites:

- As part of the event, visitors can tour Vicenza's important churches and basilicas and observe specific rituals and worship of the patron saint.

Colorful Parades:

- Exuberant parades and pageants enliven the streets with music, dance, and happy revelry, fostering a festive mood that brings the neighborhood together in celebration.

Activities at the Event:

Join the Procession:

- Guests have the option to take part in the religious procession, strolling side by side with locals and sharing in the joy and celebration.

Observe Local Traditions:

- Get a true sense of the culture by taking in the elaborate costumes, ceremonies, and customs that have been loved for years.

Enjoy the Pageantry:

- Take in the colorful parades and pageants that perfectly capture the festival's festive spirit and rich cultural heritage.

Attend Special Religious rituals:

- If available to the public, attending special religious rituals can give you a better understanding of the Festa della Madonna Bruna's historical significance as well as its religious significance.

The Festa della Madonna Bruna is a well-known event that highlights Vicenza's rich religious tradition and cultural legacy. This vibrant festival promises an unforgettable and enriching trip into the core of Vicenza's religious and cultural character, whether you're looking for a spiritual experience or want to take part in the city's vibrant traditions.

Venetian Carnival

The Vicenza Carnival is a vibrant and jubilant celebration that erupts in color, masks, and merriment in Vicenza, Italy. The carnival is a time for locals and visitors to gather together in celebration, embracing the spirit of joy and festivity. It is rooted in centuries-old customs.

Event date:

- The Vicenza Carnival typically occurs in February or March, however the precise dates change every year. The best place to find the current year's schedule is on the official carnival website or local event listings.

Attendee Attractions:

Colorful Masks and Costumes:

- The carnival is renowned for its colorful masks and outfits, with participants donning elaborate and creative disguises that fill the streets with a kaleidoscope of hues.

Street Parades and Floats:

- Excited crowds, music, and dance are all present as lively parades with elaborately decorated floats wind through the city.

Masked Balls and Parties:

- During the carnival season, there are masked balls and gatherings where guests can dance the night away in an enchanted setting of mystery and good times.

Art works and decorations throughout the city are themed around the carnival, which heightens the joyous atmosphere.

Things to do at the Event:

Participate in the Parades:

- Visitors can get involved in the fun by marching in the parades or by just supporting the masked participants onlookers.

Put on a Mask:

- Enter the fanciful world of carnival disguises by donning a mask or costume and getting into the carnival atmosphere.

Try classic carnival goodies like frittelle, sweet fried pastries, and other delectable bites that are offered at food vendors all around the city.

Participate in Carnival activities:

- Participate in the many carnival activities, such as masked balls and parties, where you may dance, mingle, and soak in the carnival's merry spirit.

A beloved local custom, the Vicenza Carnival brings the city to life with its jubilant revelry and artistic masks. This joyous event offers a chance to embrace the carnival spirit, honoring solidarity, creativity, and the shared happiness of this enthralling Italian culture, whether you're a local or a guest.

Chapter 6

Vicenza's Culinary Delights

Vicenza is a city rich in history and culture that is well-known for both its magnificent buildings and its delectable cuisine. Vicenza's food is a beautiful fusion of traditional Italian flavors and regional delicacies, and it is located in the Veneto region of Italy. The city offers a gourmet trip that tantalizes the taste buds and leaves food connoisseurs wanting more, from savory entrees to scrumptious desserts.

1. Traditional Venetian Cuisine:

Due to Vicenza's proximity to the Venetian Lagoon, the city offers a wide variety of traditional Venetian foods. The focus is on seafood, and two regional specialties are sarde in saor and risotto al nero di seppia, which is made with squid ink.

2. Baccalà alla Vicentina:

This traditional Vicenza dish, which is made with dried and salted fish stewed with onions, milk, and anchovies, is a true culinary gem. For seafood enthusiasts, this tasty and delicate fish dish is a must-try.

3. Polenta:

Made from coarsely ground cornmeal, polenta is yet another adored culinary institution of the Veneto region. It frequently serves as a side dish and goes well with heavy meat sauces and rich stews.

4. Asiago cheese:

Vicenza is particularly well-known for its Asiago cheese, a tasty and adaptable cheese made in the nearby mountainous regions. Try it melted over polenta, in risotto, or just by itself with regional wines.

5. Veneto Wines:

Vicenza provides the chance to sample some of the best wines from the Veneto area, which is known for its wines. The city's wine scene complements its culinary delights with robust reds like Amarone and Valpolicella and crisp whites like Soave.

6. Sopressa Veneta:

If you like meat, you must try sopressa Veneta. Garlic and red pepper are used to season this traditional Venetian salami, creating a flavorful and aromatic treat.

7. Bigoli:

A popular pasta dish in Vicenza is bigoli, a type of thick, long pasta prepared from whole wheat flour. It delivers a hearty and fulfilling meal experience and is frequently served with sauces made of duck or anchovies.

8. Tiramisu:

No visit to Vicenza would be complete without indulging in the national dessert of Italy, tiramisu. It's a delectable delicacy for sweet tooths made with layers of mascarpone cheese and ladyfingers dipped in coffee.

9. Markets for Fresh Produce:

Visit Vicenza's lively markets to find a bounty of fresh fruits, vegetables, and regional delicacies. The Mercato Coperto is a great place to find local goods and take in the bustling Italian market ambiance.

10. Gelato:

Finish your culinary journey with a few scoops of this popular ice cream from Italy. Vicenza is home to many gelaterias that offer a delicious selection of flavors produced with premium ingredients.

Vicenza's gastronomic delights reflect the city's love of food and its extensive cultural history. Every meal provides a window into the heart and spirit of this captivating Italian city, from ancient recipes handed down through the generations to contemporary takes on classic fare. So get ready for a delicious experience that captures the spirit of Italian gastronomy, whether you're dining in a quaint trattoria or meandering through the picturesque streets.

A guide to traditional foods and local cuisine

The culinary scene in Vicenza is a veritable treasure trove of regional delicacies and traditional Italian dishes that entice food lovers to set out on a delicious culinary adventure. The city's food is a celebration of fresh ingredients, rich flavors, and time-honored recipes passed down through generations. It is steeped in history and influenced by its Venetian roots. Here is a detailed guide to Vicenza's cuisine, including a list of must-try regional specialties and the ingredients, approximate cooking times, and cooking techniques for each dish:

1. Baccalà alla Vicentina (Preparation Time: 1 hour)

Ingredients:

500g dried and salted cod (baccalà)

2 large onions, thinly sliced

1 cup milk

6-8 anchovy fillets

Olive oil

Flour (for dusting)

Black pepper

Preparation Method:

1. Rinse the dried cod under cold water to remove excess salt. Place it in a large bowl of cold water and let it soak for at least 24 hours, changing the water every 6-8 hours.

2. After soaking, drain the cod and pat it dry with paper towels. Cut it into large pieces, about 4 inches wide.
Dust the cod pieces with flour, shaking off any excess.

3. In a large pan, heat some olive oil over medium heat. Add the sliced onions and sauté until soft and translucent.

4. Push the onions to the side of the pan and add the floured cod pieces. Cook on each side until lightly browned.

5. Pour in the milk and add the anchovy fillets. Season with black pepper.

6. Reduce the heat, cover the pan, and let the cod simmer in the milk for about 45 minutes or until it becomes tender and easily flakes with a fork.

7. Serve hot, drizzling some of the milk and onions over the cod.

2. Bigoli con L'Anatra (Preparation Time: 30 minutes)

Ingredients:

400g bigoli or thick spaghetti

400g duck meat, cooked and shredded

1 onion, finely chopped

2 cloves garlic, minced

1 cup tomato passata

1/2 cup red wine

Fresh thyme and rosemary

Grated Parmesan cheese

Salt and black pepper

Olive oil

Preparation Method:

1. Cook the bigoli or thick spaghetti in a pot of salted boiling water until al dente. Drain and set aside.

2. In a large pan, heat some olive oil over medium heat. Add the chopped onion and garlic, and sauté until they become fragrant and translucent.

3. Add the shredded duck meat to the pan and cook for a few minutes, allowing the flavors to meld.

4. Pour in the red wine and let it reduce slightly. Then add the tomato passata, fresh thyme, and rosemary. Season with salt and black pepper to taste.

5. Let the sauce simmer for about 15 minutes to allow the flavors to develop.

6. Toss the cooked bigoli or spaghetti in the duck sauce until well coated.
Serve hot, sprinkled with grated Parmesan cheese.

3. Risotto al Nero di Seppia (Preparation Time: 40 minutes)

Ingredients:

300g Arborio rice

500ml fish broth

1/2 cup dry white wine

400g fresh squid, cleaned and cut into rings

1 onion, finely chopped

2 cloves garlic, minced

2 tablespoons squid ink

Fresh parsley

Olive oil

Salt and black pepper

Preparation Method:

1. In a large pan, heat some olive oil over medium heat. Add the chopped onion and garlic, and sauté until they become fragrant and translucent.

2. Add the Arborio rice to the pan and toast it for a couple of minutes, stirring constantly.

3. Pour in the dry white wine and let it simmer until it evaporates.

4. Gradually add the fish broth to the rice, one ladleful at a time, stirring continuously. Allow the rice to absorb the broth before adding more.

5. Continue adding the fish broth and stirring until the rice is creamy and cooked al dente.

6. In a separate pan, sauté the squid rings in olive oil for a few minutes until they are tender.

7. Add the squid ink to the rice and stir until the risotto turns black and acquires a rich flavor.

8. Season with salt and black pepper to taste. Sprinkle with chopped fresh parsley before serving.

4. Sarde in Saor (Preparation Time: 20 minutes)

Ingredients:

500g fresh sardines, cleaned and filleted

1 cup white wine vinegar

1 cup white wine

1/2 cup raisins

1/4 cup pine nuts

2 large onions, thinly sliced

2 tablespoons sugar

Flour (for dusting)

Olive oil

Salt and black pepper

Preparation Method:

1. Rinse the sardine fillets under cold water and pat them dry with paper towels. Lightly dust them with flour, shaking off any excess.

2. In a large pan, heat some olive oil over medium heat. Fry the sardine fillets in batches until they are golden brown on both sides. Remove them from the pan and set aside.

3. In the same pan, add the thinly sliced onions and sauté until they become soft and caramelized.

4. Add the white wine vinegar, white wine, raisins, and pine nuts to the pan. Season with sugar, salt, and black pepper.

5. Simmer the mixture for a few minutes to let the flavors blend.

6. Layer the fried sardine fillets in a glass dish, alternating with the onion mixture.

7. Let the dish marinate in the refrigerator for at least a few hours or overnight before serving. The flavors will meld and develop over time.

5. Polenta e Osei (Preparation Time: 1 hour)

Ingredients:

250g coarse yellow cornmeal

1 liter water

Salt

Assorted small game birds (thrushes, quails, etc.)

2 cups meat broth

1 onion, finely chopped

2 cloves garlic, minced

Fresh herbs (thyme, rosemary, sage)

Olive oil

Salt and black pepper

Preparation Method:

1. In a large pot, bring the water to a boil. Add salt to taste.

2. Gradually pour the coarse yellow cornmeal into the boiling water, stirring constantly to prevent lumps from forming. Keep stirring until the polenta thickens and starts to pull away from the sides of the pot. This will take about 40-45 minutes.

3. While the polenta is cooking, prepare the small game birds. Clean them thoroughly and pat them dry with paper towels. Season with salt and black pepper.

4. In a separate pan, heat some olive oil over medium heat. Add the chopped onion and garlic, and sauté until they become fragrant and translucent.

5. Add the seasoned small game birds to the pan and cook until they are browned on all sides.

6. Pour the meat broth into the pan with the small game birds and bring it to a simmer. Add fresh herbs like thyme, rosemary, and sage for added flavor.

7. Let the birds simmer in the broth until they are cooked through and tender. The cooking time will depend on the type and size of the birds.

8. Once the polenta is ready, transfer it to a large serving dish. Create a well in the center of the polenta and arrange the cooked small game birds around it.

9. Pour the broth from the pan over the polenta and birds, allowing the flavors to meld.

10. Serve hot, savoring the delightful combination of creamy polenta with the succulent and flavorful small game birds.

6. Tiramisu (Preparation Time: 30 minutes)

Ingredients:
200g ladyfingers (savoiardi)
250g mascarpone cheese
3 large eggs, separated
4 tablespoons sugar
1 cup strong coffee, cooled
Cocoa powder for dusting

Preparation Method:

1. In a bowl, beat the egg yolks with the sugar until the mixture becomes creamy and pale yellow.

2. Add the mascarpone cheese to the egg yolk mixture and stir until well combined, creating a smooth and velvety cream.

3. In a separate bowl, beat the egg whites until stiff peaks form. Gently fold the beaten egg whites into the mascarpone mixture to create a light and airy texture.

4. Pour the cooled strong coffee into a shallow dish. Dip each ladyfinger into the coffee, soaking them briefly on both sides. Do not over-soak, as the ladyfingers may become too soggy.

5. Arrange a layer of soaked ladyfingers in a serving dish or individual glasses.

6. Spread a layer of the mascarpone cream over the ladyfingers, creating a smooth and even layer.

7. Repeat the process, adding more layers of soaked ladyfingers and mascarpone cream until the dish is filled, finishing with a layer of mascarpone cream on top.

8. Cover the dish with plastic wrap and refrigerate for at least a few hours, allowing the flavors to meld and the tiramisu to set.

9. Before serving, dust the top with cocoa powder, creating an enticing finishing touch.

As you immerse yourself in Vicenza's local cuisine and traditional dishes, you'll discover the heart and soul of this enchanting Italian city. From seafood delicacies to hearty pasta dishes, every bite tells a story of a region with a deep appreciation for its culinary heritage. So, whether you're dining in a quaint trattoria or sampling street food at a local market, let the flavors of Vicenza awaken your senses and leave you with cherished memories of Italy's delectable culinary delights.

Top restaurants

Il Molo

Il Molo is a pleasant and well-known restaurant serving delicious cuisine to locals and guests alike. It is situated in the center of Vicenza. This restaurant boasts a prime position close to Piazza dei Signori and an appealing atmosphere that makes it the perfect choice for an unforgettable dining experience.

Culinary Excellence: Il Molo takes great delight in offering the best traditional Venetian and Italian dishes, which are painstakingly made using the freshest ingredients from nearby sources. Every palette will like the restaurant's menu, which is a fascinating fusion of traditional dishes and cutting-edge culinary inventions.

The restaurant's menu, titled "A Symphony of Flavors," features a wide range of dishes that honor the regional flavors of the Veneto. Every bite is a symphony of genuine Italian sensations, from delicate seafood specialities like Baccalà Mantecato (creamy salted cod) to robust pasta dishes like Bigoli con Salsa (thick spaghetti with anchovy and onion sauce).

Highlight meals: The Risotto al Nero di Seppia, a visually arresting and enticing squid ink risotto studded with soft squid rings, is one of Il Molo's must-try meals. The exquisite Trittico di Baccalà, a trio of salted cod dishes, features a lovely range of flavors and textures that highlight the adaptability of this well-liked seafood.

An enchanting atmosphere is created by the restaurant's attractively decorated environment, which combines rustic and modern features. The cozy atmosphere created by the warm lighting, exposed brick walls, and wooden accents is ideal for a romantic supper or a fun get-together with friends and family.

An amazing wine selection that has been expertly crafted is available at Il Molo, and it goes nicely with the food. The restaurant provides a variety of options that appeal to both seasoned wine drinkers and casual lovers, ranging from regional Veneto wines to well-known Italian names.

Observant Service:

Service that is attentive and welcoming is a top priority at Il Molo. The crew takes great delight in giving customers a fantastic dining experience, making sure that every need is catered to with the utmost expertise and attention.

It is advised to make a reservation in advance to guarantee a table at this popular dining location given its popularity, especially during high seasons.

A magical gastronomic tour of Vicenza and the Veneto area is provided by Il Molo. This restaurant is certain to leave a lasting impression with its delicious cuisine, pleasant environment, and great service, whether you are a food enthusiast eager to sample classic Italian recipes or a connoisseur seeking culinary excellence. In Vicenza's historic center, Il Molo offers diners the chance to sample the very best of Italian cuisine while making priceless memories.

Address: Contra Pedemuro San Biagio 48, 36100 Vicenza
Italy

Phone: +39 328 808 7598

Cuisines

Italian, Healthy, Sicilian, Southern-Italian

Special diets

Vegetarian Friendly, Gluten Free Options

Meals

Dinner

Features

Reservations, Seating, Serves Alcohol, Accepts American Express, Accepts Mastercard, Accepts Visa, Accepts Credit Cards, Table Service

Fuori Modena

A hidden gem that takes customers to the culinary wonders of Emilia-Romagna is Fuori Modena. This renowned restaurant offers both locals and visitors a distinctive and unforgettable dining experience by bringing the genuine flavors of Modena to Vicenza.

Fuori Modena is renowned for its dedication to displaying the best foods from the Emilia-Romagna region. Emilia-Romagna's Culinary Treasures. Emilia-Romagna is renowned for producing some of Italy's most iconic foods, including Parmigiano-Reggiano cheese, classic aged prosciutto, balsamic vinegar, and other delicacies.

Fuori Modena's cuisine pays respect to the "art of Italian simplicity," where each dish is meticulously selected with an emphasis on premium ingredients and flawless preparation. As traditional recipes are presented with a contemporary twist, expect a harmonious blending of flavors that will captivate the senses.

Must-Try meals: The Tagliatelle al Ragù, a traditional Emilian pasta dish prepared with homemade egg noodles and served with a substantial and rich meat sauce, is one of the restaurant's must-try meals. The Tortellini en Brodo, which are small pasta packages stuffed with flavorful meats and served in a flavorful broth, is another standout.

Balsamic Brilliance: Fuori Modena's dedication to quality extends to its assortment of balsamic vinegars, which are acquired from the best Modena-based producers. No matter if they are drizzled over salads, grilled meats, or even desserts like panna cotta, the balsamic choices enhance the dining experience.

Elegant Ambiance: The restaurant's ambiance is a sophisticated blend of modern design and old-world charm. Fuori Modena is the perfect choice for a refined get-together with friends or a romantic meal because of the warm and welcoming surroundings that provide an intimate setting.

Wine Selection: Fuori Modena has an amazing wine selection that features both local and regional labels to go along with the gastronomic delights. The skilled staff can make the ideal pairing suggestion to improve the eating experience even further.

Service with Attention: Fuori Modena takes great satisfaction in offering each client attentive, personalized service. Throughout their eating experience, customers are made to feel welcome and well-cared for by the committed personnel.

It is advised to make a reservation in advance in order to guarantee a table at this renowned restaurant due to its rising popularity. In the center of Vicenza, Fuori Modena is a paradise for foodies looking for an authentic flavor of Emilia-Romagna.

A trip to Fuori Modena offers a memorable dining experience, whether you are a fan of Italian food or are just anxious to discover this region's culinary gems. Enjoy every taste of the culinary wonders of the area as you immerse yourself in the flavors of Modena and create cherished memories of a truly exceptional dining experience in Vicenza.

Address: Contra San Gaetano Thiene 8, 36100 Vicenza Italy

Website: http://www.fuorimodena.it

Price range

$6-$30

Cuisines

Italian, Mediterranean, Emilian, Northern-Italian

Meals

Dinner, Drinks

Features

Reservations, Seating, Wheelchair Accessible, Serves Alcohol, Wine and Beer, Accepts Mastercard, Accepts Visa, Accepts Credit Cards, Table Service

Antico Guelfo

The classic Italian restaurant Antico Guelfo is a shining example of how the fine skill of cooking has been scrupulously preserved and passed down through the centuries. This renowned restaurant has earned a loyal following from both locals and tourists looking for an authentic taste of the area's culinary heritage thanks to its warm and welcoming atmosphere.

Preservation of the Culinary Heritage: Antico Guelfo takes great delight in upholding the venetian and vicenza culinary traditions. Italian gastronomy's passion to excellence is reflected in the restaurant's focus to employing locally and freshly sourced ingredients.

A Symphony of tastes: Diners can expect a symphony of tastes at Antico Guelfo, where each dish is lovingly prepared to highlight the essence of the ingredients. Every dish on a plate is a celebration of Italian culinary excellence, from hearty pasta dishes to luscious meat and seafood delicacies.

Risi e Bisi, a traditional Venetian dish of creamy-perfect rice and peas, is one of the restaurant's signature dishes. A dish from the Veneto region called Brasato al Amarone, which is tender beef cooked in Amarone wine, is also a must-try.

Step inside Antico Guelfo's lovely environment to experience its quiet, intimate setting made possible by the rustic appeal of its exposed brick walls and wooden beams. Every customer feels at home because to the restaurant's excellent service and welcoming staff, which improves the whole eating experience.

Wine Selection: Antico Guelfo offers a carefully chosen wine selection that includes some of the best wines from the Veneto and beyond as a tribute to the region's rich viticulture. Each wine pairs well with the menu, enabling diners to choose the ideal beverage to go with their meals.

A gourmet Journey: Antico Guelfo welcomes visitors to take a gourmet tour of Vicenza's rich cultural and culinary history. Each dish is expertly prepared and constructed, offering a taste of genuine Italian cuisine that is memorable.

It is advised to make a reservation in advance to ensure a table at Antico Guelfo given its ubiquity and devoted clientele, particularly during busy eating hours.

More than merely a dining establishment, Antico Guelfo is evidence of the lasting allure of Italian culinary customs.

This restaurant embodies Vicenza's culinary spirit, from the cozy and welcoming atmosphere to the delectable dishes on the menu. Antico Guelfo encourages visitors to sample the traditional joys of Italian cuisine in the heart of Vicenza and delivers a true sense of the region's culinary heritage for those seeking an authentic and unforgettable dining experience.

Address: Contra Pedemuro San Biagio 92, 36100 Vicenza Italy

Phone: +39 0444 547897

Price range

$30 - $50

Cuisines

Italian, Mediterranean

Special diets

Vegetarian Friendly, Vegan Options, Gluten Free Options

Meals

Lunch, Dinner

Features

Reservations, Seating, Highchairs Available, Wheelchair Accessible, Serves Alcohol, Wine and Beer, Accepts

Mastercard, Accepts Visa, Accepts Credit Cards, Table Service, Digital Payments, Free Wifi, Dog Friendly

Angolo Palladio Restaurant

A gastronomic marvel that honors the city's rich history and magnificent architecture is Ristorante Angolo Palladio. This respected restaurant, which is situated next to the famous Palladian Basilica, is a haven for residents and discriminating visitors looking for a gourmet dining experience that skillfully combines history and modernity.

Ristorante Angolo Palladio draws inspiration from the city's famed architect, Andrea Palladio, and incorporates his ideas of proportion, balance, and harmony into its culinary creations. The cuisine at this restaurant are created with painstaking attention to detail and presentation, just as Palladio's structures are praised for their ageless elegance.

A Symphony of Flavors: Traditional Venetian and Italian cuisine are upgraded with a modern twist on the menu at Ristorante Angolo Palladio. Diners travel through a world of flavors at this restaurant, where the finest flavors and freshest ingredients are showcased in every mouthful.

Signature meals: The Risotto al Radicchio e Gorgonzola, a delectable risotto delicately imbued with the tastes of radicchio and the richness of Gorgonzola cheese, is one of the outstanding meals. Ossobuco alla Milanese, a Milanese classic of succulent braised veal shanks topped with a delicious gremolata, is another dish you must try.

Stepping into Ristorante Angolo Palladio is like entering an elegant environment that conveys both comfort and sophistication. The beautiful decor creates an intimate ambiance that is ideal for a romantic supper or a classy event with its soft lighting and attractive furnishings.

Service: Ristorante Angolo Palladio's helpful and polite personnel improves the whole dining experience. They are always prepared to make recommendations and take care of each guest's preferences thanks to their extensive knowledge of the cuisine and wine choices.

Wine Selection: An excellent array of regional and Italian wines are featured on the well crafted wine list, which perfectly complements the gastronomic delights. The wines here, which range from crisp whites to robust reds, improve the dining experience and offer an added level of pleasure to each meal.

Ristorante Angolo Palladio not only enchants guests with its delicious cuisine, but it also provides a culinary voyage through the illustrious history of the city. Visitors are encouraged to appreciate the essence of Vicenza's cultural and culinary legacy with every bite.

It is advised to make a reservation in advance to guarantee a table at Ristorante Angolo Palladio because it is a popular eating location in Vicenza, particularly during busy times.

Conclusion: Ristorante Angolo Palladio is an unrivaled option for those looking for a dining experience that flawlessly combines art, architecture, and gastronomy. This restaurant provides a window into Vicenza's essence, where the past and present coexist in a seamless celebration of culinary skill, with its exquisite cuisine, gorgeous setting, and first-rate service. A trip to Ristorante Angolo Palladio offers the chance to experience the finest Italian cuisine while taking in the beauty of the city's architecture.

Address: Piazzetta Andrea Palladio 12 Piazzetta Andrea Palladio, 12, 36100 Vicenza Italy

Website: http://www.angolopalladio.it

Phone: +39 0444 327790

Cuisines

Italian, Pizza, Seafood, Mediterranean, European

Special diets

Vegetarian Friendly, Vegan Options, Gluten Free Options

Meals

Lunch, Dinner, Brunch

Features

Reservations, Outdoor Seating, Seating, Highchairs Available, Wheelchair Accessible, Serves Alcohol, Full Bar, Free Wifi, Accepts Credit Cards, Table Service

Da Biasio's Restaurant

A gastronomic landmark that has delighted guests for years is Ristorante Da Biasio. With a distinguished history spanning more than a century, this fine restaurant continues to wow both locals and guests with its authentic Italian fare, welcoming atmosphere, and first-rate service.

A Culinary Legacy: Since 1882, Ristorante Da Biasio has contributed to Vicenza's culinary scene, and its continued success is evidence of its dedication to culinary quality. The restaurant proudly showcases the delicacies of the Veneto region by putting a special emphasis on preserving time-honored recipes and employing the freshest seasonal ingredients.

An Authentic Dining Experience: Entering Ristorante Da Biasio is like stepping through a time vortex into the past, where tradition and authenticity are king. The attractive rooms have a warm and nostalgic atmosphere thanks to its old furnishings, soft lighting, and typical Italian charm.

Signature meals: The restaurant's menu features a wide selection of specialty meals that exemplify the best of Italian cooking. A must-try is the Risotto con Radicchio e Gorgonzola, a thick risotto flavored with the distinctive flavors of radicchio and Gorgonzola cheese. The Tagliata di Manzo, a tender beef steak topped with flavorful herbs and a drizzle of extra virgin olive oil, is another favorite.

Service: The attentive and kind employees at Ristorante Da Biasio make sure that each customer is treated like a member of the family. They work hard to make each dining experience memorable and delightful out of a true passion for hospitality.

Wine collection: To go with the delicious food, there is a carefully chosen wine list that includes an amazing collection of Italian wines. Each course's ideal pairing is suggested by the experienced sommeliers, further improving the dining experience.

A Celebration of Tradition: Ristorante Da Biasio is more than just a dining establishment—it's a working example of

Vicenza's rich culinary history. Diners engage on a gastronomic adventure that honors the region's culinary heritage as they experience the genuine flavors and time-honored recipes.

It is advised to make a reservation in advance to guarantee a place at Ristorante Da Biasio given its illustrious history and devoted clientele, particularly during busy times and on weekends.

Ristorante Da Biasio is a superb option for anyone looking for a memorable dining experience rooted in tradition and culinary creativity. Immerse yourself in the restaurant's rich legacy and history while you appreciate the wonderful cuisine. When you dine at Ristorante Da Biasio, you may experience the very best of Italian cuisine and leave with priceless memories of an unforgettable dining experience right in the middle of Vicenza.

Address: Viale Dieci Giugno 172, 36100 Vicenza Italy
Website: http://www.ristorantedabiasio.it
Phone: +39 0444 323363

About: Closed on Mondays, On Saturdays opens for Dinner only

Price range

$20-$50

Cuisines

Italian, Seafood, Mediterranean, European

Special diets

Vegetarian Friendly, Vegan Options, Gluten Free Options

Meals

Lunch, Dinner, Late Night

Features

Reservations, Outdoor Seating, Private Dining, Seating, Parking Available, Validated Parking, Valet Parking, Highchairs Available, Wheelchair Accessible, Serves Alcohol, Full Bar, Accepts Credit Cards, Table Service

Chapter 7

Vicenza's Shopping Delights

Vicenza, also provides a great shopping experience that appeals to all tastes. Vicenza's shopping scene is a treasure trove for fashion fans, art lovers, and connoisseurs of exquisite craftsmanship, with everything from opulent stores to charming local markets.

Chic boutiques and clothing companies:

- The major shopping street, Corso Palladio, is dotted with stylish stores and fashion houses that display the most recent styles in both Italian and global fashion. You can engage in a shopping binge befitting a fashion aficionado at any number of high-end establishments, which offer everything from known designer labels to chic accessories. Although the stores normally open at 10:00 AM and close at 7:30 PM, it's always a good idea to double-check each location's hours in case there are any changes.

Craftsmanship Treasures:

- Vicenza's artisanal boutiques are a great joy for anyone looking for one-of-a-kind and handcrafted things. These artisanal businesses offer one-of-a-kind items that reflect the city's creative past, from delicate jewelry made with excellent goldwork and influenced by the city's goldsmithing tradition to lovely ceramics and leather goods.

Regional Markets:

- The unique and charming atmosphere of Vicenza's local markets enhances the shopping experience. The Mercato delle Sogni, or Market of Dreams, is a weekly market that takes place every Saturday along Piazza dei Signori. Here, you may find a wide variety of goods, from locally produced food to handcrafted crafts. The market has a bustling atmosphere that is ideal for exploring and finding hidden jewels. It begins early in the morning and closes in the afternoon.

Shopping Centers:

- Vicenza has a number of shopping malls where you can find a variety of worldwide brands and local merchants if you prefer a more contemporary shopping experience. These malls normally open at 9:00 AM and end at 8:00 PM, giving you plenty of time to window shop and indulge your every whim.

Antiques and vintage finds:

- Vicenza's antique shops provide a fascinating journey through history for antique lovers and collectors. Find one-of-a-kind vintage items for your house, such as collectibles and furniture, that give it personality and a sense of history.

Gastronomic delights:

- Without partaking in some of Vicenza's culinary treats, no shopping trip is complete. Treat yourself to delicious chocolates, handcrafted gelato, or rich local wines, which all make excellent keepsakes to remember your time in Vicenza by.

Nighttime shopping:

- The city occasionally holds "Notte Bianca," or White Night, where stores and boutiques stay up into the wee hours of the morning to provide a lovely and joyous shopping experience.

Shopping advice for Vicenza:

1. Plan your afternoon shopping properly because many stores take a short break for the customary siesta.

2. As some smaller stores and markets might not accept credit cards, bring cash.

It's normal in Italy to barter at the local markets, so don't be shy about doing so.

Vicenza's shops offer a mesmerizing fusion of modern beauty and age-old workmanship. The city's varied shopping environment guarantees to satisfy all of your needs, whether you're looking for fashionable clothing, handmade goods, or genuine souvenirs. Step into Vicenza's lovely streets, peruse the shops and markets, and set off on a shopping excursion to discover the genuine spirit of this shopping paradise.

Mercato di Vicenza

T he vibrant and genuine Mercato di Vicenza is a market that captures the true spirit of Italian culture and cuisine. For years, locals and tourists have flocked to this ancient market because it provides a sensory thrill and an opportunity to get a sense of Vicenza's vivacious personality.

A Mixture of Aromas and Flavors:

- Mercato di Vicenza welcomes you with a beautiful symphony of hues, scents, and noises as soon as you enter. The market offers a wide variety of fresh food, including fruits and vegetables from the neighborhood, savory herbs, and handmade cheeses that highlight the local cuisine.

Seasonal and Local Delights:

- The market takes pleasure in providing the finest seasonal and local dishes from the Veneto region.

The market is a gold mine for food connoisseurs looking for genuine Italian products, offering Prosciutto di San Daniele, famous Grana Padano cheese, as well as olives, oils, and delicious Baccalà.

A feast of fresh seafood:

- The vibrant seafood area of the market will enthrall seafood aficionados. Fresh seafood from the adjacent Adriatic Sea, such as delectable shrimp, octopus, and the well-known Adriatic anchovies, are abundant here.

Craftsmanship Treasures:

- The market offers more than just food; it also features a beautiful selection of handmade items and crafts. The great tradition of workmanship in the area is celebrated via handcrafted pottery, fabrics, exquisite jewelry, and other one-of-a-kind items.

Times and Days of the Market:

- Every Thursday and Saturday from the wee hours of the morning until close to 1:00 PM, Mercato di Vicenza is hosted on the charming Piazza dei Signori. The market is at its liveliest when you arrive, and the produce and seafood are at their freshest.

What to Do to Have a Memorable Market Experience:

Get There Early:

Arrive early in the morning to avoid the crowds and explore the market when it is at its busiest.

Attempt Local Delights:

As you browse the market, don't forget to try some of the local specialties and street food options.

Bring money:

It's essential to carry cash because not all stalls have card facilities, even though some vendors may accept credit cards.

Engage the Community:

Engage the amiable merchants in conversation to embrace the atmosphere of the neighborhood market. They frequently enjoy sharing anecdotes and advice.

The Mercato di Vicenza provides a true and comprehensive look into the center of Italian society. You may take in the bright flavors, find artisanal gifts, and experience Vicenza's welcoming and pleasant environment as you stroll through the market. A trip to this historic market ensures that visitors will have an unforgettable, authentic Italian market experience that embodies the spirit of the community. Soak up the market's joys, adopt the customs of the area, and make treasured memories of Vicenza's gastronomic wonders and cultural diversity.

Souvenirs

Vicenza offers a lovely selection of mementos that you may use as reminders of your amazing trip to Italy. Whether you're looking for vintage knickknacks, handcrafted goods, or gourmet treats, the city's collection of mementos perfectly portrays the spirit of this alluring location.

1. Filigree and gold jewelry

Vicenza is the ideal location to find magnificent gold jewelry and delicate filigree items because it is the world's foremost center for goldsmithing. Discover exquisitely created necklaces, earrings, and bracelets that perfectly capture the city's goldwork legacy by exploring the neighborhood jewelry stores.

2. Custom-made ceramics

The excellent selection of hand-painted ceramics available at Vicenza's handmade ceramic shops ranges from colorful tiles and plates to endearing figurines. These one-of-a-kind items make beautiful ornamental keepsakes that capture the creative allure of the city.

3. Leather Products

Another notable aspect of Vicenza's artisanal heritage is leather craftsmanship. Look for premium leather wallets, belts, handbags, and other accessories that highlight the local artists' skillful handiwork.

4. Italian masks

Vicenza has a sizable collection of Venetian masks, and Venice is only a short distance away. These ornately adorned masks are fascinating and distinctive keepsakes that capture the joyous atmosphere of Italy's most well-known carnival.

5. Balsamic vinegar bottles:

The renowned Modena region, known for producing balsamic vinegar, lies near to Vicenza. Invest on a bottle of old balsamic vinegar, known for its delectable flavor and adaptability in the kitchen.

6. Italian cuisine:

Enjoy delicious treats from Vicenza's local markets, including artisanal chocolates, aromatic herbs, extra-virgin olive oil, and regional wines. These tasty trinkets serve as a tantalizing remembrance of Italian cuisine.

7. molten glass

Despite not being local to Vicenza, some stores sell Murano glass from the nearby city of Venice. Beautiful Murano glassware, such as jewelry, vases, and ornamental objects, makes for a priceless keepsake.

Shopping Advice for Souvenirs:

Encourage artisans:

Look for regional artisanal stores and marketplaces to obtain genuine and one-of-a-kind souvenirs that help the area's artisans.

Test the quality:

Before making a purchase, check the item's quality and craftsmanship to make sure you're getting mementos that are representative of the city's artistic talent.

Watch Out for Items Made in Mass:

Avoid purchasing mass-produced souvenirs as they may lack the charm and originality of handmade items.

Time of Opening and Closing:

Vicenza's markets and gift stores normally open at or around 9:00 AM and close at or around 7:30 PM. It is best to call ahead to confirm the specific business hours because they may change.

Vicenza's mementos provide a material reminder of your unforgettable Italian adventure. Immerse yourself in the craftsmanship of regional crafts and delicacies that embody the cultural character of this stunning region as you stroll through the city's picturesque streets. To convey the atmosphere of Italy with loved ones back home and to bring back cherished memories of Vicenza's ageless charms, choose souvenirs with care.

CHAPTER 8

Outdoor Adventures and Activities

Vicenza provides a variety of outdoor pursuits and excursions that appeal to both nature lovers and thrill seekers. This charming city offers the ideal location for experiencing nature and making lifelong experiences because it is surrounded by rolling hills, vineyards, and historical sites.

Vicenza's outdoor pursuits and experiences offer the ideal fusion of the beauty of nature and cultural diversity. The area promises an exciting voyage through breathtaking landscapes and treasured moments of calm, whether you're looking for exhilarating adventures or peaceful discoveries. Take advantage of the outdoors' allure and immerse yourself in Vicenza's magical adventures.

Discover the Beauty of Nature:

Explore the amazing natural splendor that surrounds Vicenza by venturing beyond the city's architectural highlights. The area provides a variety of scenery just begging to be explored, from tranquil lakes and twisting rivers to lush green slopes.

Trails for hiking and trekking

With its charming hiking and trekking trails, Vicenza, a city rich in history and culture, offers a nice surprise for outdoor enthusiasts. The area invites travelers to explore its wild beauty on foot because it is surrounded by thick vegetation, rolling hills, and beautiful views. Put on your hiking boots and go out on a memorable tour through Vicenza's breathtaking scenery.

Every Explorer's Trail

Vicenza offers a wide variety of paths for hikers of all skill levels, accommodating both experienced trekkers and leisurely walkers. The area has plenty to offer any traveler, whether they are looking for a tranquil stroll through nature's embrace or an adrenaline-pumping ascent.

Old Forests and Beautiful Valleys:

Explore the depths of ancient forests where the earthy scent of moss permeates the air and sunlight streams through thick canopies. Wander through picturesque valleys on trails while looking out for wildflowers that brighten the surroundings with their blooms.

Stunning Views from High Peaks:
People looking for dramatic views should visit the region's high peaks for breathtaking sights. Conquer the difficulties of climbing rocky terrains, and you'll be rewarded with breath-taking views that reach far into the distance.

Find Undiscovered Gems:
Vicenza's hidden treasures are revealed via hiking and walking there. Discover tranquil lakes, bubbling streams, and beautiful villages tucked away in the lush surroundings. Each route promises a special journey that reveals the area's natural wonders.

Accept the Seasons
Vicenza's hiking attractions shift with the seasons, giving a variety of experiences all through the year. Witness the awakening of nature in the spring as flowers and leaves begin to bloom. Warm breezes and rich greenery are

available in the summer, while colorful foliage covers the pathways in the fall. Snow-capped summits give the region a wonderful atmosphere in winter, transforming it into a tranquil wonderland.

Advice for Vicenza Hiking:

Proper equipment

Don't forget to take a daypack with essentials like water, snacks, and a map, as well as sturdy hiking shoes and weather-appropriate clothing.

Keep hydrated

Carry enough water to last the duration of your hike, especially on warmer days.

Trail conditions to check

Before beginning any trip, pay attention to the weather forecast and the state of the trail.

Observe nature

By leaving no evidence of your visit and respecting the wildlife and vegetation, you can preserve the beauty of the paths.

Vicenza's hiking and trekking opportunities provide a unique opportunity to get in touch with nature, allowing you to get away from the bustle of the city and lose yourself in the tranquil embrace of the great outdoors. Discover the hidden wonders that make this area a sanctuary for nature lovers as you traverse ancient woods, scale stunning peaks, and more. Discover the natural beauty that compliments Vicenza's cultural attractiveness with each step, and make treasured memories of an adventure that will never be forgotten.

Routes for biking and cycling

Cycling enthusiasts and casual riders alike are drawn to Vicenza's picturesque countryside, which offers a network of alluring routes that promise an amazing experience on two wheels. Enjoy the freedom of the open road as you cruise through orchards, vineyards, and quaint villages, taking in the natural beauty of the area.

Get Ready for Beautiful Rides:

Vicenza offers a variety of cycling routes that are suitable for riders of all skill levels, whether they are experienced or novice. Every bicycling enthusiast can find the perfect track, from easy strolls to difficult adventures, all of which promise delightful surprises along the way.

Rolling Hills and Vineyards:

Ride through the renowned Veneto region's vineyards in gorgeous fashion. Enjoy the cool rural air as you pedal through mild hills that pass lush vineyards and take in the idyllic beauty of the surroundings.

Citrus Groves and Aromatic Meadows:

The aroma of ripe fruits fills the air as you cycle through fragrant orchards, while the countryside is painted in a rainbow of hues by blooming meadows. Enjoy the peace and quiet of the countryside as you stroll amid all of nature's splendor.

Quaint towns and historical sites:

As you travel by bicycle through quaint towns, it feels as though time has stopped. While cycling, take time to explore historical locations and admire the architecture from the past.

Waterside Views and Riverside Trails:

Explore the paths along rivers that lead to tranquil views and tranquil waters. Find the ideal location to take a calm break by the water's edge as you pedal by streams that are glistening with water.

Cycling Routes That Are Family-Friendly:

Family-friendly cycling routes offer a delightful day of bonding amidst the marvels of nature to families with young children. Enjoy leisurely rides through parks and meadows while creating priceless memories.

Cycling Advice for Vicenza:

Rent bicycles:

If you don't already possess a bicycle, think about renting one from a local company that offers a selection of bikes suited to various terrains and preferences.

Verify Routes:

Select routes based on your riding tastes and skill level, and always check the state of the trails before you head out.

Keep hydrated and eat regularly:

Bring snacks and drinks with you when riding, especially on longer trips, to stay hydrated and energized.

Observe local laws:

Observe traffic laws, and show consideration for other drivers, pedestrians, and bicycles.

Vicenza's cycling and biking opportunities provide an unmatched opportunity to get in touch with the natural beauty and rural charm of the area. You'll discover Vicenza's natural beauty as you cycle through vineyards, orchards, and ancient towns, which perfectly compliment the city's cultural treasures. Explore the beautiful countryside on two wheels as you embrace the joy of riding, feel the wind in your hair, and make lifelong memories. Whether you're a serious cyclist or just enjoy riding your bike for fun, Vicenza's cycling routes offer an amazing trip that honors the age-old appeal of nature.

Sports and Thrills for Adventure

Vicenza's wild terrains and rocky landscapes provide a variety of heart-pounding activities for thrill-seekers and adventurers that guarantee an exhilarating rush unlike anything other. This magical area invites adventurers to set out on risky journeys that will leave them feeling thrilled and yearning for more, whether they involve flying through the skies or scaling dangerous cliffs.

Soar Like a Bird with Paragliding:

Experience the freedom of flight while gliding over Vicenza's stunning surroundings by taking to the sky with a paraglider. Your sense of floating above the earth as beautiful landscapes unfold below will leave you in awe and make you feel closer to the wonders of nature.

Climbing rocks:

Succeed in Vertical Heights:

Rock climbers of all ability levels are drawn to Vicenza's precipitous cliffs and rocky formations to hone their techniques and scale great heights. The area offers a range of routes and climbing sites to suit different levels, whether you're an experienced climber or a beginner looking to try this exhilarating sport.

Canyoning:

Go down into the Hidden Gorges:

Canyoning is a thrilling activity that involves rappelling down waterfalls, swimming through natural pools, and navigating through breathtaking canyons. It allows you to explore Vicenza's secret gorges and waterways. With this action-packed activity, you may see some of the area's most remote and captivating places.

Glide with the Wind: Zip Lining

Try zip lining among the treetops for an exhilarating flying adventure. Fly across ravines and through dense forests as you enjoy the thrill of flying through the air. You'll feel the wind in your hair.

Mt. Bike riding

Take on Difficult Terrain:

Vicenza's mountain biking trails guarantee an exhilarating ride through difficult terrain. Set out on exhilarating trails that meander through untamed terrain and provide an energizing blend of speed, skill, and scenic beauty.

Adventure Sports in Vicenza Recommendations:

Priority One:

Put safety first by getting expert advice and wearing the right gear for each adventurous activity.

Select Licensed Providers:

Select adventure sport providers with qualified instructors and solid safety records.

Consider the Environment:

While on your expeditions, be mindful of the environment and the wildlife, taking care to leave no traces of your presence.

Vicenza offers an unrivaled opportunity to test your limits, embrace adrenaline, and connect with the unadulterated beauty of nature through adventure sports and thrills. Whether you choose to fly paragliding over breathtaking vistas, rock climbing up craggy cliffs, or canyoning through undiscovered gorges, each activity promises to be life-changing and unforgettable. Vicenza's natural playground beckons you to leave your comfort zone, enjoy the thrill, and make priceless memories of daring adventures in the enchanted countryside of Italy.

Water Sports

Vicenza's natural attractions go beyond its picturesque surroundings and include a range of water sports that entice both adventure seekers and those looking to unwind by the sea. The area provides a plethora of aquatic experiences that beckon you to jump in and immerse yourself in the cooling embrace of nature, from calm lakes to mild rivers.

Glide Along Calm Waters: Kayaking and Canoeing

By kayaking or canoeing, you may explore Vicenza's lakes and rivers while gliding over tranquil waters that perfectly capture the splendor of the surrounding scenery. These waterways guarantee a peaceful and restorative journey, regardless of how much experience you have paddling.

Paddleboarding: Discover Harmony and Peace:

A stable board allows you to stand above motionless lakes or meandering rivers and paddle across them, providing a unique perspective of Vicenza's waters. Enjoy the feeling of tranquility and equilibrium that comes with flying over calm water.

Cruises and Boating: A Relaxing Getaway

Spend some time on one of Vicenza's tranquil lakes with a boat trip or cruise for a relaxing aquatic getaway. Enjoy the beautiful scenery as you float along the water's edge while listening to the waves gently lap against the boat.

Recreational Swimming: Cool Off in Natural Pools

Visit one of the many natural swimming areas that dot Vicenza's terrain for a relaxing swim. You are invited to relax and take in the peace of nature by the lakes and rivers that are crystal pure.

Cast a Line and Relax While Fishing:

Vicenza's waters provide good opportunity to cast a line and wait for a catch for those who appreciate the sport of fishing. The lakes and rivers in the area are teeming with fish, making fishing a tranquil and meditative activity.

Tips for Vicenza Water Activities:

Always put safety first by donning the proper protective gear and adhering to all water activity safety rules.

Respect wildlife: Be aware of the surrounding surroundings and the aquatic creatures.

Check the Weather: Before starting any water-based expedition, keep an eye on the weather forecasts.

Vicenza's water activities offer a revitalizing and energizing method to interact with the aquatic wonders of nature. Whether you're paddling in a kayak, taking a leisurely boat ride, or just having a dip in the natural pools, these experiences provide an opportunity to relax, recharge, and make priceless memories amidst the area's stunning scenery. Take advantage of Vicenza's appeal for water activities and allow the calm of the city's waters to surround you in a delightful embrace of the natural world's splendor.

Explorations of History

The historical riches of Vicenza stretch far beyond the city limits, luring history buffs on intriguing excursions that combine the charm of the outdoors with the riches of the past. Explore historic fortifications from the Middle Ages, castles from the Renaissance, and archaeological sites as you become immersed in the illustrious past of the area.

Fortresses and castles: Reminders of the Past

Visit the antique fortresses and castles that dot Vicenza's countryside by setting off on a historical excursion. Exploring them offers a window into the life of folks who once resided in these impressive structures and serves as a witness to the turbulent history of the area.

Visiting Archaeological Sites to Discover Ancient Mysteries

There are numerous archaeological sites in the region surrounding Vicenza that provide insight into earlier civilizations. Discover unique antiques, Roman ruin fragments, and old settlement relics as you peel back the layers of the region's history.

Historic Walks & Trails: Trace the Steps of the Past

Wander through the countryside on historic routes and ancient paths to follow in the footsteps of historical figures. As you interact with the same landscapes that have witnessed the passage of time, these walks provide a distinctive perspective on the history of the area.

Quaint towns with cultural heritage:

The rural communities surrounding Vicenza are rich in history and include quaint streets and distinctive buildings from bygone centuries. Discover the picturesque cathedrals, ancient squares, and cobblestone alleys that represent the local culture.

Legacy of Palladius:

Vicenza is famed for its exquisite architecture, and Andrea Palladio's creations have left a lasting impression on the cityscape. As you make your way out into the countryside, you'll come across mansions and palaces created by the master architect that combine historical and artistic marvels.

Advice for Vicenza Historical Excursions:

Study and Plan:

Study the historical locations you want to see, then organize your tours appropriately.

Honor cultural heritage:

Respect the cultural significance of historical places and settlements when you visit them, and abide by any visitation regulations that may be in place.

Travel with a Guide:

Take into account joining expert-led excursions that are led by knowledgeable locals who can add fascinating historical background and make your visit more memorable.

Vicenza's historical excursions offer a mesmerizing synthesis of the natural beauty and the area's cultural magnificence. You will have a greater understanding of the rich historical fabric that has defined Vicenza's identity as you explore medieval castles, follow historical trails, and visit archaeological sites. Take advantage of the chance to travel back in time as you connect with the past among the everlasting attraction of nature. These historical journeys guarantee an educational and unforgettable excursion through Vicenza's intriguing past.

Picnics and leisure

Vicenza offers a tranquil respite for those seeking moments of leisure and connection with nature amid the bustling metropolis and historical attractions. Visitors can enjoy the simple pleasures of life by going on picnics in beautiful locations, soaking up the sun, and relaxing by the calm waters of the area's lakes and rivers, to name just a few lovely outdoor activities.

Pick a Beautiful Location: Nature's Dining Room

The countryside surrounding Vicenza is dotted with charming locations that make the ideal backdrop for an enjoyable picnic. Whether it's a verdant meadow, a shady woodland, or the shores of a tranquil lake, these places transform into nature's dining rooms and invite you to indulge in regional specialties amidst the alluring surroundings.

Local Delights: Outdoor Culinary Activities

Try some of Vicenza's culinary treats to make your picnic experience even better. Local delicacies like artisanal cheeses, freshly baked bread, cured meats, and locally grown fruits can be packed in a picnic basket to make a feast that matches the surrounding scenery.

Unwinding by the Water: A Refreshing Interlude

Vicenza's lakes and rivers provide serene retreats. Spread out a blanket along the water's edge and allow the soothing sounds of the lapping waves and the cold breeze calm your body and mind. Put your feet in the cool water or just enjoy the tranquil atmosphere of these natural havens.

Unplug and relax. Adopt a digital detox.

Picnics in Vicenza's green spaces offer a chance to disconnect from technology and re-establish relationships with family and friends. Put your electronics away and enjoy life's simple pleasures while concentrating on the beauty of your surroundings and the delight of shared experiences.

Family-friendly Activities: Make Treasured Memories

Vicenza picnics are ideal for family vacations and making priceless memories. Children may play in the middle of the beauty of nature, discovering the great outdoors and taking part in activities that encourage a love of the natural world.

Tips for Relaxation and Picnics in Vicenza:

Bring the necessities: To keep your picnic environmentally friendly, bring a picnic blanket, reusable plates, cutlery, and trash bags.

Carry a lot of water with you to stay hydrated, especially on warm days.

Respect nature by taking all trash with you and leaving no sign of your picnic in order to keep the area's unspoiled beauty.

In Vicenza, picnics and leisure time provide an opportunity to unwind, take in the fresh air, and discover tranquillity amidst the area's natural havens. These easy outdoor activities encourage a closer connection with nature and a restorative break from the rapid pace of life, whether you're indulging in regional specialties, relaxing by the sea, or making priceless family memories. Accept the allure of Vicenza's picnics and leisure time, and allow the alluring atmosphere of the outdoors to embrace you in moments of delightful tranquility.

CHAPTER 9

Day Trips and Nearby Attractions

Vicenza is the perfect starting point for a variety of exciting day trips and neighboring attractions. There are several lovely locations nearby this charming city, each having its own special charm and cultural richness. Explore the rich tapestry of neighboring attractions that are waiting to be discovered just outside Vicenza's boundaries as you set off on a journey through history, art, and natural grandeur. Every curious traveler may expect an enriching and fascinating experience from the region's day tours, whether they are looking for historic towns, imposing mountains, or tranquil lakes.

Verona

A day journey from Vicenza to Verona promises to be a magical adventure filled with history, romance, and architectural marvels. Verona, which is around 60 kilometers (37 miles) distant, entices with its enduring attractiveness and association with Shakespeare's famous play "Romeo and Juliet."

Best Mode of Transportation:

- The best mode of transportation for a day excursion from Vicenza to Verona is by rail. With frequent connections between the two cities, trains provide a practical and effective form of transportation. The trip takes about one and a half hours, giving you plenty of time to discover Verona's wonders.

Coverage of Travel Time:

- It is advised to allot at least 6 to 8 hours in Verona for a relaxed day excursion. With this amount of time, you can leisurely take in the city's attractions and atmosphere.

Things to Do in Verona

- Every traveler is enthralled by the abundance of historical sites and cultural treasures in Verona. Some attractions that are a must-see are:

Arena di Verona (Verona Arena):

One of the best preserved amphitheaters in the world is the Arena di Verona, a former Roman amphitheater. Admire its splendor and picture the gladiatorial shows that formerly took place on its stage.

House of Juliet (Casa di Giulietta):

- Explore the setting of Shakespeare's "Romeo and Juliet" play at Juliet's House, where guests leave love notes on the walls and look for the fabled balcony.

Square of the Erbe:

- Piazza delle Erbe is a bustling plaza filled with medieval structures and a bustling market that emanates historic charm and provides a lively scene for wandering and people-watching.

Bridge of Pietra

- Cross the renowned Ponte Pietra, a Roman stone bridge across the Adige River that provides breathtaking views of Verona's riverbank architecture.

Things to do in Verona:

There are lots of enjoyable activities to partake in while visiting Verona aside from sightseeing:

Exploring the Old Town

- Get lost in Verona's old center's tiny lanes and streets as you take in the city's magnificent architecture and medieval atmosphere.

Veronese cuisine to try:

- Enjoy delicious dishes from Verona like risotto, pastissada (braised horse flesh), and Amarone wine.

Get on a riverboat:

- A leisurely sail along the Adige River offers a special vantage point from which to view Verona's famous attractions.

Castelvecchio excursion:

Explore the magnificent castle that serves as the museum for the amazing art collections at the medieval Castelvecchio.

A day excursion from Vicenza to Verona offers a travel through history where romance, culture, and history all meld together. Verona's appeal guarantees an amazing experience, whether you choose to explore ancient amphitheaters or reenact the Romeo and Juliet story. Immerse yourself in this Shakespearean city's charm, and let its alluring beauty leave you with lifelong memories.

Padova, or Padua

As you explore the wonders of this charming Italian city, a day excursion from Vicenza to Padua offers a delightful tour through history and culture. Every curious traveler may expect a memorable experience in Padua because to its rich history, beautiful architecture, and lively atmosphere.

Train is the best mode of transportation.

Train travel is the most practical and effective way to get from Vicenza to Padua. Regular train service between the two cities offers a relaxing and beautiful experience.

Duration of the journey:

About 30 to 40 minutes

A short and hassle-free day trip, the train ride from Vicenza to Padua takes about 30 to 40 minutes.

Mileage Traveled:

The equivalent of 40 kilometers

Vicenza and Padua are separated by around 40 kilometers (25 miles).

Things to see in Padua

(Cappella degli Scrovegni) Scrovegni Chapel

Admire Giotto's breathtaking frescoes, which are unquestionably a masterpiece of Western art.

Prati of the Valley:

Discover one of Europe's largest squares, which is surrounded by opulent architecture and is embellished with statues.

Saint Anthony's Basilica (Basilica di Sant'Antonio):
Visit the majestic basilica that houses Saint Anthony of Padua's bones.

Università degli Studi di Padova (University of Padua):
Take a stroll through one of the oldest university campuses in the world.

Della Ragione Palace
Discover this magnificent medieval town hall with its enormous wooden roof.

Things to do in Padua:
Visit the Piovego Canal via Gondola:
Take a leisurely gondola ride through the picturesque Piovego Canal.

Go to the Padova Botanical Garden (Orto Botanico):
Experience one of the oldest botanical gardens in the world's splendor.

Look around the Market District:

Visit the bustling marketplaces like Piazza delle Erbe and Piazza della Frutta to sample the fresh local fare.

Climb Torre dell'Orologio, the Clock Tower:

Atop the clock tower, you may get a bird's-eye perspective of Padua's cityscape.

Eat some Italian food:

Eat traditional trattoria fare including pasta, risotto, and gelato to experience the regional cuisine.

An educational journey that reveals the historical and cultural gems of this intriguing city is a day trip from Vicenza to Padua. Padua offers an immersive experience that will leave you with priceless memories, from artistic wonders to lovely squares and bustling marketplaces. So board a train and embark on an exciting adventure to discover Padua's alluring allure.

(Venezia) Venice

A day excursion to the enchanted city of Venice is a must-do adventure if you're staying in Vicenza. Travelers from all over the world are drawn to Venice by its distinctive architecture, tranquil canals, and rich history. Here is some advice for maximizing your visit to Venice during the day:

Train is the best mode of transportation.

Train travel is the most practical and effective way to get from Vicenza to Venice. Between the two cities, regular rail service runs, offering a smooth and comfortable ride. The train ride lasts around an hour and provides a beautiful view of the Veneto region's landscape.

Time Spent:

Vicenza to Venice and return takes about 2 to 3 hours by rail, giving you plenty of time to see the main attractions in Venice in a single day.

Mileage Traveled:

Vicenza and Venice are separated by around 80 kilometers (50 miles).

Places to Visit in Venice

Piazza San Marco, also known as St. Mark's Square

St. Mark's Square, the center of Venice, is surrounded by breathtaking construction, including the Campanile (bell tower) and St. Mark's Basilica. Admire the basilica's façade's beautiful features, then climb the Campanile for a stunning view of the city.

Bridge at Rialto:

The Rialto Bridge, one of Venice's most recognizable structures, spans the Grand Canal and provides stunning views of the river and the busy markets below.

Palace of the Duke (Doge's Palace):

Discover the lavish Doge's Palace, which served as the former home of the Venetian aristocracy. Explore the opulent spaces, which are filled with exquisite artwork, and discover Venice's political past.

Big Canal:

Observe the beautiful architecture that lines the Grand Canal by taking a vaporetto (water bus) journey along it.

Islands of Burano and Murano:

Think about taking a quick boat ride to Burano, an island known for its colourful homes and lace-making heritage. Or go to Murano to see the traditional craft of glassblowing in action.

Things to do in Venice:

Gondola Tour:

A gondola ride through the city's congested canals is a must-do for anybody visiting Venice, and it's a beautiful and fascinating way to see the city.

Venice's Special Ambience

With its charming canals, ancient bridges, and magnificent architecture, Venice is unlike any other city in the world. A calm and pedestrian-friendly environment is created by the absence of cars and busy roadways, which promotes leisurely exploration.

Italian cuisine

During your day tour, indulge in the mouthwatering flavors of Venetian cuisine. The city's gastronomic offerings are a feast for the senses, with everything from succulent seafood delicacies like risotto al nero di seppia (black squid ink risotto) to sweet pleasures like fritelle (Venetian doughnuts).

Local Craftspeople and Gifts:

You'll come across a lot of artisan shops and workshops as you stroll through Venice's lovely streets. Take advantage of the chance to buy genuine Murano glassware, delicate lace, and hand-made masks, each of which is an example of Venetian artistry.

Gelato Treats:

Without enjoying some gelato, a journey to Italy is not complete. The numerous gelaterias dotted throughout Venice are a great place to treat yourself to a scoop or two of creamy, delicious gelato.

Collections Ca' d'Oro with Peggy Guggenheim:

The Ca' d'Oro is a magnificent palace that houses an extensive collection of artwork that spans several centuries. The Peggy Guggenheim Collection features an exceptional selection of 20th-century masterworks for fans of modern art.

Sunset Views and a Boat Tour:

If you want to see Venice from a different angle, think about taking a boat trip of the outer islands. Find a beautiful location to watch the romantic Venetian sunset over the lagoon as the day draws to a close.

Discover Small Squares and Streets:

Get lost in Venice's entrancing appeal as you meander around the maze-like streets and discover secret squares.

Trip Advice:

Leaving early:

Consider taking an early train from Vicenza to Venice to get the most out of your day vacation.

Shoes that are cozy:

When exploring the bridges and cobblestone streets of Venice, wear comfortable shoes.

Make a plan:

To make the most of your time in Venice, order the sights and experiences you want to encounter.

The ageless allure and cultural gems of one of the world's most alluring cities may be seen on a day excursion from Vicenza to Venice. Make memories that will last a lifetime by soaking up the environment, tasting the cuisine, and experiencing the charm of Venice.

Let Venice's ageless beauty and romantic allure leave you with priceless memories as you enjoy your day trip there!

Bel Grappa, Bassano

S et out on a magical day excursion from Vicenza to the alluring Italian village of Bassano del Grappa, which is tucked away in the Veneto area. This charming location is only a short drive away and offers a lovely getaway rich in history, culture, and beautiful scenery.

Best Mode of Transportation:

Train travel is the most practical mode of transportation for a day journey from Vicenza to Bassano del Grappa. The train ride takes about 30 to 40 minutes, and it offers a quick and pleasant way to get where you're going.

Time Spent:

Spending many hours in Bassano del Grappa during a day trip gives you plenty of time to see the town's top sights and take in its quaint atmosphere.

Distance cover:

Vicenza and Bassano del Grappa are separated by a distance of roughly 30 km (18.6 miles).

Visitor Attractions in Bassano del Grappa

Alpine Bridge (Alpini Bridge):

This famous wooden bridge across the Brenta River provides sweeping views of the city and its surroundings.

Don't pass up the chance to meander through this old building.

Alpine Museum (Museo degli Alpini):
Learn about the historical significance of the Alpini, an elite mountain infantry unit of the Italian Army. The museum displays relics and souvenirs from their exploits.

Visit the Duomo di Bassano (Bassano church):
A stunning church with a striking exterior and imposing interiors decorated with priceless works of art.

Museum of the City (Museo Civico):
At the Civic Museum, you may explore the history, art, and culture of the community via a wide variety of exhibits.

Distilleries of grappa:
The grappa that bears its name is famous in Bassano del Grappa. Learn about the manufacturing process and try various variations of this traditional Italian liqueur during a tour of a nearby distillery.

Things to do in Bassano del Grappa:

Explore the town's lovely streets, which are dotted with artisan shops where you can buy one-of-a-kind crafts, trinkets, and handmade goods.

Eat local food:

Enjoy authentic Italian cuisine at neighborhood trattorias and eateries. Remember to sample some regional delicacies like risotto, polenta, and local cheeses.

Explore Piazza della Libertà:

The center of Bassano del Grappa, this busy plaza is teeming with cafes, shops, and a dynamic ambiance.

Enjoy the Views:

Visit one of the town's magnificent lookout sites, such the panoramic terrace close to the Alpini Bridge, to take in the mesmerizing views.

Discover the vibrant artistic community in Bassano by visiting the area's galleries and workshops.

A day excursion to Bassano del Grappa from Vicenza is a lovely opportunity to discover the attractiveness and charm of this captivating Italian town. Just a short drive from Vicenza, Bassano del Grappa offers a great getaway with its historical sites, cultural hubs, and natural beauty.

CHAPTER 10

Travelers' Practical InformationItinerary for Vicenza

Itinerary for One Day: Highlights Tour

Morning:

- Start each day at Vicenza's central Piazza dei Signori. Enjoy the Palladian Loggia and the stunning Palladian Basilica.

- Learn more about the creations of legendary architect Andrea Palladio by visiting the Museo Palladio.

Mid-Morning:

- If one is offered, have a tour of the spectacular Renaissance theater Teatro Olimpico by walking there.

- Investigate Chiesa di Santa Corona, a venerable church with stunning artwork.

Lunchtime:

- At a nearby trattoria or osteria, have a typical Italian meal. Consider trying some local delicacies like risotto alla Vicentina.

Afternoon:

- Drive a short distance from the city center to Villa Rotonda to see Palladio's masterpiece surrounded by lovely gardens.

- Visit Villa Valmarana ai Nani, which is renowned for its beautiful sculptures and frescoes.

Evening:

- Go back to the city's core and wander down the elegantly decorated Corso Palladio.

- Ponte San Michele is a charming bridge with beautiful views, a great place to end the day.

Itinerary for three days: exploration of culture and nature

Day 1:

- Focus on the city's architectural highlights and landmarks as you travel the one-day tour.

- Visit Palazzo Thiene, another Palladian masterpiece, and Palazzo Chiericati, a Renaissance palace that houses the Civic Museum.

Day 2:

- Visit the nearby city of Padua (Padova), which is renowned for its ancient university, the Basilica of Saint Anthony, and the Scrovegni Chapel.

- Discover one of the oldest botanical gardens in the world.

- Return to Vicenza in the evening for a leisurely meal.

Day 3:

- For a lovely drive and beautiful views of the surroundings, visit the Berici Hills.

- Visit the Palladian-designed Villa La Rotonda (Villa Almerico Capra), which is a UNESCO World Heritage site.

- Spend the afternoon at the serene lake, Lago di Fimon, which is surrounded by the outdoors.

Itinerary for One Week: Immersive Experience

Day 1-4:

- Follow the three-day plan, stopping at each of Vicenza, Padua, and the Berici Hills' top sights.
- Visit Vicenza's Teatro Olimpico to see a performance or another cultural event.

Day 5-6:

- Visit Verona for the day; it is known for Juliet's balcony and the Arena di Verona, a Roman amphitheater.

Visit the Piazza delle Erbe and Piazza dei Signori in the old center.

Day 7:

- A day trip to nearby Venice (Venezia) is recommended. Take a gondola ride, see the beautiful canals, and proceed to St. Mark's Square and Basilica.
- Before going back to Vicenza, savor some authentic Venetian cuisine at a nearby restaurant.

Note that you can adjust this schedule to fit your interests and pace. To gain a better knowledge of the historical and cultural value of each location, think about signing up for guided tours. Always confirm the availability and hours of operation before making travel arrangements.

How to Get Around Vicenza

Walking: Vicenza is a walker-friendly city, so getting around on foot is the ideal way to experience its quaint atmosphere. Walking is a quick and entertaining choice because the majority of the city's top sights, businesses, and eateries are concentrated in the city center.

Bicycles: To get around the city more effectively, think about hiring a bicycle. Vicenza is a bicycle-friendly city with designated bike lanes and accessible bike-sharing programs. When you bike, you may travel farther while taking in the scenery and the fresh air.

Buses: ACTV operates a reliable public bus system in Vicenza. Numerous neighborhoods and the neighboring areas are connected by buses. Tickets can be bought at specific kiosks or onboard the ship.

Taxis and ride-sharing services are widely available in Vicenza, especially in the areas close to well-known tourist attractions and transportation hubs. Uber and other ride-sharing services are available for quick travel.

Transport Outside Vicenza

Trains: Thanks to Vicenza's advantageous position, there are several Italian cities that are easily accessible by rail. Vicenza Railway Station, the city's train station, acts as a significant center for both national and regional trains. A convenient and effective way to see surrounding cities like Venice, Verona, Padua, and Milan is by rail.

Buses & Coaches: Regional and long-distance bus services connect Vicenza to the nearby local towns and tourist destinations. Travelers looking to leave the city have handy options from businesses like FlixBus and Eurolines.

Renting a car gives you more freedom and flexibility as you explore the Veneto region. Vicenza is home to a number of vehicle rental companies, and major motorways offer quick access to nearby cities and scenic scenery.

Joining guided tours for day outings and excursions to neighboring destinations is a good idea. Tour companies provide well-planned itineraries that take care of all logistics and transportation issues.

Practical Advice

Consider getting the Venezia Unica City Pass, which grants access to public transportation and cultural venues in Venice and the Veneto region, if you intend to travel to Venice or other surrounding cities.

Train Ticket Validation: Before boarding a train, make sure you validate your tickets. There could be consequences if the validation is not done.

Check the Public Transportation Schedules: Especially for early morning or late-night trips, confirm the bus and train schedules in advance.

Plan for Traffic: If you're driving, pay attention to the traffic, particularly during rush hours and on holidays.

Discover Car-Free Zones: Keep in mind that some of Vicenza's historic districts either don't allow cars at all or have very limited access to them.

Travelers can have smooth and effective travel inside Vicenza and beyond by being knowledgeable about transportation alternatives, assuring a memorable and gratifying time taking in the cultural and natural treasures of the Veneto region.

Tips for health and safety

1. Number for emergencies

Get to know the crucial emergency numbers in Italy. 112, which links to police, fire, and medical aid, is the general emergency number. You may also call 118 in cases of medical emergencies.

2. Travel Protection:

Make sure you have adequate travel insurance before you leave, which should cover medical emergencies, trip cancellations, and lost or stolen property. Store a copy of your insurance information nearby.

3. Keep hydrated:

Keep yourself hydrated by drinking lots of water throughout the day, especially during the warmer months.

Bring a reusable water bottle with you and keep an eye out for the closest public water faucets for quick access.

4. Medications on prescription:

Make sure you have enough prescription medication for the duration of your vacation if you're bringing any. Keep them in their original, transparent container, and always have a copy of your prescription on you.

5. Security in Public Areas:

Vicenza is generally secure, however use caution in congested locations. Be cautious with your possessions and stay away from flashing expensive goods like jewelry or cameras in popular tourist areas.

6. Using Sunscreen:

Use sunscreen with a high SPF, sunglasses, and a hat with a wide brim to prevent sunburn on sunny days. When the sun is most intense (10 am to 4 pm), seek shade.

7. Water and Food Safety:

Italian food is delicious, but to prevent foodborne infections, only eat at recognized restaurants. Drink only bottled water; stay away from untreated sources.

8. Scams and robberies:

In crowded areas, be on the lookout for frauds and pickpockets, especially near tourist hotspots and transportation hubs. Secure your belongings, and stay away from those who seem off-putting.

9. Medical Emergency Services:

Excellent medical services, including hospitals and clinics, are available in Vicenza. Call emergency services or go to the closest hospital for help in the event of a medical emergency.

10. Observe regional customs:

Be mindful of regional traditions and culture, particularly while visiting places of worship or taking part in community activities. When entering churches and other places of worship, dress modestly.

11. Language Disparity:

Despite the fact that English is frequently spoken in tourist regions, learning a few simple Italian words can improve your travels and make conversation easier.

You can completely enjoy your trip to Vicenza and create priceless memories while discovering the city's rich history, cultural treasures, and natural beauty by putting your health and safety first. To guarantee a safe and pleasurable journey, always stay informed and adopt the appropriate safety measures.

Emergency numbers

Keeping Safe During Your Visit to Vicenza: Emergency Contacts

It's crucial to have access to emergency contacts when visiting Vicenza in order to secure your safety and wellbeing. To manage any unforeseen events as soon as possible, become familiar with these crucial figures and facts.

Call the emergency services hotline at (112) if there is a medical, police, or fire emergency. By dialing this number, you can reach the main emergency response center, where operators can send the proper help to your location.

Medical Emergencies:

- To request an ambulance in the event of a medical emergency, dial 118. To deliver quick aid, the operators will collaborate with the neighborhood medical services.

You can contact the Tourist Police (Polizia Turistica) at +39 800 006776 for non-emergency help, inquiries, or support pertaining to tourism. They can offer details on security, local laws, and tourism attractions.

Police (Polizia di Stato):

- You can reach the Polizia di Stato by phoning 113 if you come across any criminal activity or need police help.

Fire Department (Vigili del Fuoco): To contact the Vigili del Fuoco in case of a fire emergency, dial 115.

Civil Protection (Protezione Civile):

- For assistance and information in times of civil emergencies or natural catastrophes, call Protezione Civile at 800 840 840.

A hospital or other medical facility

- Vicenza's primary hospital, Ospedale San Bortolo, is situated at 37 Via Rodolfi. Telephone: +39 0444 75 1111.

Pharmacy: In Vicenza, pharmacists post a list of after-hours emergency pharmacies. Find the closest one or ask for help at your hotel.

Important Advice

To make emergency calls, ensure sure your mobile device is charged and has a local SIM card or an international roaming plan.

Maintain a copy of your passport, information on your travel insurance, and critical medical records with you at all times.

Establish a meeting place if you are traveling with a group or family in case you become separated in congested regions.

Make a note of the location's address and phone number so you may give it to rescue personnel if necessary.

By keeping these emergency numbers close at hand, you can travel to Vicenza with assurance, knowing that you are well-equipped to manage any unforeseen circumstances that may happen, ensuring a safe and enjoyable experience while you are there.

Daily Budget

To ensure a relaxing and pleasurable stay in Vicenza, it is essential to comprehend and organize your daily spending. With some careful planning, you may maximize your trip without going over budget. The city offers a variety of options to suit different budgets. Here is a thorough guide to aid you in estimating your daily costs:

Accommodation:

Budget Accommodation: Hostels and guesthouses with basic individual rooms or shared dorms can be found for between $20 and $50 per night.

Mid-Range Accommodation: For an average nightly cost of between €70 and €120, mid-range hotels and bed & breakfasts provide additional comfort and amenities.

Luxurious Accommodations: Luxurious hotels and boutique lodgings can cost anything from €150 to €300 or more per night for upscale experiences.

Meals:

Budget between €5 and €10 for a basic breakfast at a bakery or café.

Lunch: choose a trattoria or food cart where meals may be had for between €10 and €15.

Dinner: Treat yourself to a good dinner at a nearby restaurant for between €20 and €40 per person, excluding drinks.

Drinks and Snacks: Set up an extra €5 to €10 for coffee, soda, and snacks throughout the day.

Activities and Sightseeing:

Entry Fees: Keep in mind that museums, historical institutions, and other attractions may charge an entrance fee of between €5 and €15 per person.

Guided Tours: If you decide to go on a guided tour, plan on spending between €20 and €40 per person for a group tour and more for a private trip.

Transportation

Local Transportation: A single trip on Vicenza's effective bus system costs about €1.50. For frequent travelers, day passes or multi-ride tickets are more cost-effective options.

Day trips: Include travel expenses to nearby cities or tourist destinations in your budget. Depending on the destination, train tickets for day visits might cost anywhere from €10 and €30.

Miscellaneous:

Set aside some money to buy presents and mementos as souvenirs. Depending on one's interests and purchasing patterns, the amount fluctuates.

Budget between €5 and €10 a day for miscellaneous expenses such as tips, toiletries, and other incidentals.

Daily Budget Overall:

Budget tourists should set up between €40 and €60 per person per day, depending on their lodging and meal preferences.

Mid-Range visitors: Taking into account modest lodging and food options, mid-range visitors should budget between €80 and €150 per person per day.

Luxury Travelers: Set aside a daily budget of €200 or more per person to indulge in more opulent accommodations, exquisite meals, and other luxuries during your trip.

Practical Advice

Use cash while making little transactions because not all locations accept credit cards, particularly in more modest businesses.

For more affordable dining options, take advantage of the fixed-price lunch menus or "menu del giorno" given at numerous eateries.

Look into any municipal passes or discounts that can result in cheaper entrance fees for attractions or public transportation.

You can enjoy Vicenza to the fullest by indulging in its cultural treasures, tasting delectable cuisine, and exploring the city's ancient beauty without worrying about money if you have a well-planned daily budget.

Cultural Manners

To ensure a positive and courteous interaction with the local community when visiting Vicenza, it is crucial to comprehend and observe local cultural etiquette. Italians take great pleasure in their vibrant cultural past, and keeping in mind some of their traditions and practices will make your trip more enjoyable. Here are some essential cultural etiquette guidelines to remember:

1. Salutations and Private Space:

Italians are kind and welcoming people who frequently shake hands or give each other cheek kisses when they first meet. However, it's advisable to wait for the locals to make the first move. Keep a comfortable distance when talking to individuals and avoid getting too close, especially if you don't know them well.

2. Fashion Code:

Italians typically take care and dress attractively. While casual attire is fine for daily activities, it is welcomed when people dress more formally while entering churches or other formal locations.

In order to show respect, keep your shoulders and knees covered when visiting places of worship.

3. Punctuality:

Italians value being on time for official events and business meetings. Respecting the time and responsibilities of others is shown by arriving on time.

4. Dining Manners:

In Italy, eating is a social and relaxed activity. Take your time and savor each course of food as you enjoy it.

In spite of the fact that service fees are frequently already included in the bill, it is traditional to give a small tip (between 5% and 10%) when dining out.

It is deemed improper to request Parmesan cheese with foods like seafood pasta or risotto.

5. Communication through Language:

Respecting the local way of life might be demonstrated by learning a few simple Italian phrases.

As part of their communication style, Italians frequently make expressive hand gestures and facial expressions when speaking.

6. Bargaining and Shopping

With the possible exception of flea markets or street sellers, bargaining is uncommon in the majority of Italian stores.

Even if you don't buy anything, always be pleasant and polite when shopping.

7. Sites of Worship:

Dress decently and refrain from loud talks or disruptive conduct when visiting churches.

Visitors to some churches would need to cover their knees and shoulders. Remember the guidelines and dress appropriately.

8. Historic sites and the arts:

Respectfully handle art, museums, and historical sites. Unless specifically permitted, refrain from touching artifacts or pieces of art.

9. Gratuities and Service Fees:

A "coperto" fee that covers table service may be added to the bill at restaurants. Although not required, extra tips are gratefully accepted for truly great service.

10. Public Areas

To be considerate of others, keep noise levels down, especially in populated locations or on public transportation.
Do not leave trash lying about; always dispose of it appropriately.

Locals in Vicenza will be even more warm and appreciative of your efforts if you are aware of and respect their cultural customs. Accepting the regional customs enhances your vacation experience, promoting positive relationships and leaving you with enduring memories of this lovely Italian city.

Useful Expressions

Knowing a few simple Italian words will tremendously improve your trip to Vicenza and make interacting with locals more fun. Even though English is widely spoken in Vicenza, learning a few basic Italian phrases might help you feel more at ease while traveling and demonstrate your respect for the country's culture. Here are a few key words to get you going:

Greetings and Polite Expressions:

Hello / Hi - Ciao (chow)

Good morning - Buongiorno (bwon-jor-no)

Good afternoon / Good evening - Buonasera (bwoh-nah-seh-rah)

Goodbye - Arrivederci (ah-ree-veh-dehr-chee)

Please - Per favore (pehr fah-voh-reh)

Thank you - Grazie (graht-see-eh)

You're welcome - Prego (preh-goh)

Excuse me / Sorry - Scusa / Mi scusi (scoo-zah / mee skoo-zee)

Basic Conversation:

Yes - Sì (see)

No - No (noh)

How are you? - Come stai? / Come sta? (koh-meh stah-ee / koh-meh stah)

I'm fine, thank you - Sto bene, grazie (stoh beh-neh, graht-see-eh)

What's your name? - Come ti chiami? / Come si chiama? (koh-meh tee kee-ah-mee / koh-meh see kee-ah-mah)

My name is... - Mi chiamo... (mee kee-ah-moh)

Nice to meet you - Piacere di conoscerti / Piacere di conoscerla (pyah-cheh-reh dee koh-noh-shehr-tee / pyah-cheh-reh dee koh-noh-shehr-lah)

Directions and Transportation:

Where is...? - Dove si trova...? (doh-veh see troh-vah)

How much is this? - Quanto costa questo? (kwahn-toh koh-stah kweh-stoh)

I need a taxi - Ho bisogno di un taxi (oh bee-zoh-nyoh dee oon tahk-see)

Train station - Stazione ferroviaria (stah-tsee-oh-neh feh-roh-vee-ah-ree-ah)

Bus stop - Fermata dell'autobus (fehr-mah-tah del-aw-toh-boos)

Dining Out:

Menu - Menù (meh-noo)

Water - Acqua (ahk-kwah)

Coffee - Caffè (kahf-feh)

I would like... - Vorrei... (vohr-ray)

The bill, please - Il conto, per favore (eel kohn-toh, pehr fah-voh-reh)

Emergency Phrases:

Help! - Aiuto! (ah-yoo-toh)

I need a doctor - Ho bisogno di un medico (oh bee-zoh-nyoh dee oon meh-dee-koh)

Call the police - Chiamate la polizia (kyah-mah-teh lah poh-lee-tsee-ah)

Local Etiquette

Being polite is essential in Italian culture. Always greet with a smile and use "please" and "thank you" in interactions.

Tip: Carry a pocket-sized phrasebook or use language translation apps on your smartphone to help with pronunciation and comprehension.

By incorporating these useful phrases into your conversations, you'll find that locals in Vicenza will be even more welcoming, and you'll be able to navigate daily situations with ease, making your trip to Vicenza a truly enriching and enjoyable experience.

CONCLUSION

As we get to the end of this in-depth Vicenza travel guide, it is clear that this charming Italian city has a lot to offer tourists of all kinds. Vicenza is a place that seamlessly blends the past and the present, capturing visitors with its ageless charms thanks to its rich historical history, breathtaking architecture, and vibrant cultural scene.

An Architectural Wonderland:

Vicenza, where Andrea Palladio's architectural wonders adorn the city's environment, serves as a live example of his brilliance as an architect. Each building is a work of art, from the magnificent Basilica Palladiana to the towering Teatro Olimpico. Visitors are transported back in time to a period of opulence and ingenuity by exploring these landmarks.

A Haven for Culture:

Vicenza is known for its architectural splendors as well as its thriving cultural scene, which is highlighted by the city's museums, galleries, and theaters. The Vicenza Jazz

Festival, the Teatro Olimpico's enthralling productions, and the works of regional artists may all be fully experienced by visitors.

Foodie Pleasures:

The gastronomic treats of Vicenza are a pleasure for the senses. The city's food culture is a gastronomic trip worth experiencing, with everything from charming gelato parlors and neighborhood wine bars to classic trattorias serving delectable pasta meals. For a truly authentic dining experience, don't pass up the chance to eat regional favorites like risotto all'amarone and baccalà alla vicentina.

Outdoor adventures and the beauty of nature

The area around Vicenza has a wealth of untapped natural beauty that is just waiting to be discovered. An escape into the embrace of nature is made possible by hiking in the adjacent Berici Hills, biking along the Brenta River, or having a picnic amidst lush vegetation.

Courtesy and warmth

The kind and hospitable residents of Vicenza add to the charm of the city. The residents of Vicenza embrace the Italian tradition of hospitality, making sure that guests are made to feel welcome and have access to the city's cultural treasures.

Practical Advice for a Painless Journey:

Additionally, our travel guide offers useful details for a smooth journey, such as transit choices inside Vicenza and beyond, emergency contacts, cultural etiquette, and spending advice. With these tips in hand, visitors can easily explore the city, guaranteeing a memorable and hassle-free time.

A Story of Classic Elegance

Vicenza shows itself as a city of ageless elegance as you walk along the cobblestone streets, take in the Palladian façade, and immerse yourself in the native way of life. The heart and spirit are captured by its fusion of art, history, and modernity, creating an enduring impression on those who are fortunate enough to stroll its enchanted pathways.

Along with outstanding examples of architecture, Vicenza embodies the ethos of a city that embraces the past while embracing the contemporary. As you say goodbye to this alluring location, you'll take a treasure trove of memories and encounters with you that capture Vicenza's soul as a timeless gem in the crown of Italy's cultural legacy.

Recommendation

Consider these helpful tips while you travel to Vicenza to make the most of your stay and fully experience the city's stunning scenery and rich cultural heritage:

1. **Wander through Vicenza's Historic Center:**
   Vicenza's historic center is a UNESCO World Heritage Site, so start your journey there. Spend some time admiring the Palladian architecture, strolling along Corso Andrea Palladio and visiting famous sites like Piazza dei Signori and Basilica Palladiana.

2. Guided Tours:

    To learn more about the city's history and art, think about taking a guided tour. Local tour guides can share interesting tales and point out undiscovered attractions.

3. Go to the Teatro Olimpico:

    Don't miss the opportunity to see the Teatro Olimpico, the oldest still-operating indoor theater in the world. Discover a cultural treasure that has mesmerized audiences for ages as you awe at its exquisite trompe-l'oeil stage design.

4. Indulge in Local Cuisine:

    Visit neighborhood trattorias and osterias to sample authentic Vicenza cuisine. Try some famous regional wines like Amarone as you study the local wine culture.

5. Day Trips:

    Make the most of Vicenza's advantageous location by taking a short excursion to one of the adjacent cities, such as Verona, Padua, or Venice. Your Italian adventure will be richer thanks to the distinctive cultural assets and experiences offered by each location.

6. **Adopt Cultural Etiquette:**
To create beneficial contacts with the kind-hearted Vicentini, respect local customs and cultural etiquette. Making friends with the locals and breaking the ice can be greatly facilitated by learning a few Italian phrases.

7. **Attend Festivals and Events:**
Consult the calendar to learn about Festivals and Events taking place while you are there. Your trip's highlights can include attending the Vicenza Jazz Festival, Festa della Madonna Bruna, or Vicenza Opera Festival.

8. **Combine history and nature by exploring the natural beauties in Vicenza's vicinity:**
Explore the gorgeous hiking paths in the Berici Hills, or see the Palladian homes in the area, such Villa La Rotonda, for a perfect fusion of architecture and nature.

9. Capture Memories:

Take pictures of the stunning scenery, fascinating architecture, and energetic city life with your camera or smartphone. Vicenza provides a wealth of photo options that will ensure that your recollections are priceless.

10. Interact with Locals:

Talk to people who live there and other visitors to learn interesting insights on the area. To experience Vicenza as it truly is, strike up talks at neighborhood markets or participate in cultural activities.

11. Create a flexible agenda that allows for both exploration and downtime:
Combine relaxed time at cafes, parks, or along the Brenta River with sightseeing.

12. Seek Inspiration from the Arts:
Take in the local arts scene by visiting galleries of modern art, going to live events, or just taking in the inspiration that permeates the streets.

You can make your trip to Vicenza full of memorable experiences by paying attention to these suggestions. Accept the city's enduring fascination and allow its cultural splendors to enchant you, leaving you with a deep appreciation for this alluring Italian jewel.

Printed in Great Britain
by Amazon

28356400R00136